Born in Sydney in 1943, Rob
combined the careers of wri

is especially known for his poetry which has been published widely and translated into seven languages, including Russian and Chinese. In collaboration with Bruce Hanford, Adamson wrote a novel, *Zimmer's Essay* (1974). His own publications include *Swamp Riddles*, *Cross The Border*, *Where I Come From*, *The Law At Heart's Desire* and *Selected Poems*. Robert Adamson was instrumental in creating and editing *New Poetry* magazine, and *Prism Books*. He was editor-director, with Dorothy Hewett, of Big Smoke Books. He lives on the Hawkesbury River where, with Juno Gemes and Michael Wilding, he directs and edits *Paper Bark Press*. His last book *The Clean Dark* (1990) won three of Australia's major poetry awards, The Kenneth Slessor Award (The New South Wales Literary Award), The Turnbull Fox Phillips Poetry Prize (The National Book Council's Banjo Award) and the C.J. Dennis Prize (The Victorian Premier's Literary Award).

ALSO BY ROBERT ADAMSON

IMPRINT
lives

WARDS
OF THE
STATE

An Autobiographical Novella

ROBERT ADAMSON

Angus&Robertson
An imprint of HarperCollins*Publishers*

AN ANGUS & ROBERTSON BOOK
An imprint of HarperCollinsPublishers

First published in Australia in 1992 by
CollinsAngus&Robertson Publishers Pty Limited (ACN 009 913 517)
A division of HarperCollinsPublishers (Australia) Pty Limited
25-31 Ryde Road, Pymble NSW 2073, Australia

HarperCollinsPublishers (New Zealand) Limited
31 View Road, Glenfield, Auckland 10, New Zealand

HarperCollinsPublishers Limited
77-85 Fulham Palace Road, London W6 8JB, United Kingdom

National Library of Australia
Cataloguing-in-Publication data:

Adamson, Robert, 1943-
    Wards of the State

    ISBN 0 207 17404 0

    1. Adamson, Robert, 1943-   -Bibliography. 2. Poets, Australian-
    20th Century-Biography. 3. Juvenile delinquents-Australia-
    Biography. I. Title
A821.3

Cover photograph by Juno Gemes
Typeset in Australia by Midland Typesetters
Printed in Australia by Griffin Press

5 4 3 2 1
95 94 93 92

Orlando's book,
and my fierce wife, Juno

ACKNOWLEDGEMENTS

Grateful acknowledgement is made to the following publications, in which prose and poetry first appeared, often in very different form: the *Age*, the *Australian*, the *Canberra Times*, the Mattara/Butterfly Books Prize anthology, *Meanjin*, *Outrider*, *Overland*, *Pictures from an Exhibition*, the *Phoenix Review*, Salt, *Southerly*, the *Sydney Morning Herald*, the *Sydney Review*, and especially to the editors of *Scripsi*, Peter Craven and Andrew Rutherford, for their last-minute deadlines and editorial inspirations.

Quotations were drawn from the following editions: *Pale Fire* by Vladimir Nabokov (Penguin); *L'Abbe C* by Georges Bataille (Marion Boyars); *Things* by Francis Ponge (translated by Cid Cormon, Grossman Publishers); *The Poems of Hart Crane* (WW Norton), *Love for Sale: the words and pictures of Barbara Kruger* (Abrams), and *Opus Posthumous* by Wallace Stevens (Knopf).

I would like to thank the Literature Board of the Australia Council and the New South Wales Literary Awards, the Victorian Premier's Literary Award and Turnbull Fox Phillips (Banjo Award) for the fellowships and prizes that created the time to make this book possible.

Also, a special thanks to my wife, Juno, who not only created the photographic images, but gave her time editing and shaping this book—who made it cohere.

CONTENTS

PART ONE

CATCH THE WILDE FISHES

YOU ARE MY SUNSHINE

SEA OF HEARTBREAK

CAROL/ROBERT

CORRESPONDENCES

PART TWO

LOOSE TALK

BOATMAN OF THE GLOW

THE BIRD-CATCHER'S SONG

WARDS
OF THE
STATE

◆

PART ONE

The only way to atone for the sin of writing is to annihilate what is written. But that can be done only by the author; destruction leaves that which is essential intact. I can, however, tie negation so closely to affirmation that my pen gradually effaces what it has written. In so doing it accomplishes, in a word, what is generally accomplished by 'time'—which, from among its multifarious edifices, allows only the traces of death to subsist. I believe that the secret of literature is there, and that a book is not a thing of beauty unless it is skilfully adorned with the indifference of the ruins. Otherwise it would be necessary to shout so loudly that no one would imagine the survival of someone who bellowed so naively. That is why, with Robert dead and these ingenuous writings being left, I had to destroy this evil he had created: why, indirectly through my book, I had to annihilate, to kill him again.

GEORGES BATAILLE

L'ABBÉ C

CATCH THE WILDE FISHES

The silver strophe . . . The canto bright
with myth . . .

H A R T   C R A N E

◆

IT could almost be true: her voice, her talk, her voices. Carol, who I can't let go; the shadow of the others. In a milkbar at the top of Falcon Street in Crows Nest in 1957, Carol creating the world with a can of hairspray, standing behind me in a cloud of perfume. Carol the Max Factor Kid, smelling of musk and mascara. The black smudges under her eyelids made her black-flecked green eyes look even more sexy. Ah, she was hot, her mascara was melting. She always seemed to be moving, even when she was sitting—ruffling her plumage, hitching her skirts, three of them all worn at once, three petticoats and three reasons why. There was always something hanging loose, but right, just loose enough. What is she saying? Now it starts to seem real, here in the thick of words that could bring her back. The talk of factory jobs, hairdressing for girls or part-time at Coles, at The Big Bear, and the boys were called grease monkeys; we sold the news in the traffic or rode bikes for the chemists. Sunsets after work with sentimental parents, drunk at the table from the six o'clock swill, crying one minute and thumping you on the back of the head the next, mothers slapping faces. Out the back and a Coke with Bex, Craven A, Turfs, Seahorse cigarettes. Tuck in the shirt, shine the bloody shoes, get your mother a cup of tea. Then on the street looking for a double-malted, Four Squares and pick up the Checkers. The V8 motors revving on benches, Mercuries and Chevs with their skin paper thin from rust yet shiny as patent leather. It could almost be real,

5

talking through petrol-cracked lips, smelling of sump oil, burning around The Corso with the smell of burnt clutch pads, plates scored and the loose tappets rattling. Feeling the sunburn that summer when Carol just walked into my life, standing in the milkbar with her black hair and pissed off eyes. Coming from the jukebox, the car radio: O, Carol, I will always love you and we will never part. The strange warnings from Wolverton Mountain, with Clifton Towers, the pretty young daughter, mighty handy with that gun and a knife. Carol—who caught in the corner of my eye at The Dogs and Trots, at two-up at Thommos, her skirts swishing when she danced the Stomp. Her way of looking at you, her eyes of hate, eyes of love and spite, her head twisted and her heart wrenched, by backyard abortions, child welfare, her kid the state ward, the baby she never got to hold in her arms. Her laughter and talk, her screaming, crying and lies, the truth in her half-truths—her memories. The made-up background, her real childhood in Belfast, in Soho or Liverpool. Her coming to Australia and her father shooting through, her mother dumping her for a sailor, deserting her and her sister. O, Carol, I will always love you, sure we will never part . . . or whatever the songs were saying, Paul Anka, Ben E. King; they were true, they were all speaking the truth, they were about us. We didn't need to talk, the songs sang to each other from jukebox to jukebox; we spoke I suppose. About the songs— hey, this one's for you, this next is our song, see you at eight, play you a song, come on a date, sure, see ya round—like a record. Oh god, sure, there we were. It was all true. We were the voices, we had plenty of time. Her age, what was her age in the milkbar days in Crows Nest, she who was ageless? Her clever tricks with talk making money, money from strangers, with looks and words. Money is a kind of poetry, said the poet Wallace Stevens; for Carol, poetry was a kind of money. These thoughts are taking the place of Carol, who takes the place of my words.

Detectives and Paradise Rifle Birds

MY father rode into the school my mother attended on a white horse. He asked her if she wanted a ride; she jumped up onto the back of Rocky Ned and they galloped away, going to a nearby beach and not returning to their homes until the next morning. It was a calm, clear, hot summer night: Sydney Harbour was itchy with war, mullet splashed the glassy surface, rainbow lorikeets screeched before settling into coral trees, flying foxes streamed out from their umbrage in the great Moreton bay figs like silent black flags in the sky above Balmoral Beach. The palomino grazed in long grass by the young lovers and my life began.

My mother and father were married in 1943 and moved into a house in Neutral Bay. My father sold Rocky Ned and his other buckjumping horses and bought a sensible Clydesdale, Dobbin. Dad collected bottles in the cart and resold them to a glass company. Our backyard was large enough to house the new horse in a makeshift stable; we had long rows of vegetables—beans and potato and tomato patches, and the pumpkins and choko vines would climb up over the roof of the fowl yard. I could walk down to Neutral Bay wharf from one side of Military Road, or go down the other through Cammeray Golf Links to Primrose Park. I'd walk along the shoreline of the upper reaches of Middle Harbour to Tunks Park. At Castlecrag there is a crazy bridge that looks like a castle, the streets had names like Arthur, Merlin and Falcon. North Sydney Park had a high, red-brick chimney we called the 'Stink Pot', and down from there was an old, overgrown estate called 'Fisher's Paradise'. I haunted the shore and bushy slopes; there were huge stormwater tunnels I would explore with my friends, we would walk for what seemed like miles under Primrose Park up into Cammeray, where great dark square caves held hundreds of tiny bats clinging to the sides. There was a tram depot nearby with dark pit bays for repairing the trams, and a gas works at Lavender Bay. It was a strange paradise really for a boy with an imagination. I hunted birds, fish and bats in the tunnels of darkness at Tunks Park. It was only a short tram ride to Taronga Park Zoo—I loved it there and often ran away. I'd go to the quarantine area at Chowder Bay, an eerie place where they kept incredible animals for months before taking them into the main zoo. Night after night I'd sit there in the darkness surrounded by strange animals making unnerving sounds. I got to know exotic creatures like the cassowary, zebras, giraffes, ostriches, emus and strange reptiles like salamanders and a monster called the Komodo dragon. I terrified myself one night when I climbed up over a barbed wire fence and slipped and fell into one of the enclosures. I got up and found myself face to face with an angry cassowary. It had a furious-sounding voice, a deep, reverberating booming noise, and it hissed and drummed simultaneously. Booming and strutting, it came towards me. I knew a lot about this bird from my bird

9

book, where I read about how they had been known to disembowel men in New Guinea when provoked. I stood there utterly still, a long hour, the great black bird with its horn of a head fringed with iridescent blue feathers shivering in the moonlight. The angry bird circled around me, booming and hissing and gurgling with spite around and round. Finally, after what seemed like the longest hour of my life, it walked over to the other end of the cage and totally ignored me.

I had no idea what I was heading for in my life, but I was failing school at everything except nature studies and art. I kept pigeons—road peckers—at home, in with my father's chooks. I would take the baby squeakers from their nests and train them to home. They nested high in the gutters of old blocks of flats and two storeyed houses around Neutral Bay, and they took up most of my time. I even discovered a pigeon racing club at Mosman. There I met up with Ricky Stacy, a young apprentice jockey; Rick the Trick he was called. Rick knew some dodgy characters and through one of his mates knew the famous fence Tilly Divine. We ended up stealing, and in the end I stole birds from the zoo. Rick used to say: 'How can anyone own a bird? They are part of nature—if anyone owns them it would have to be God if he exists.' He'd say things like that, I was impressed. It made the kind of sense I wanted to hear.

One night I fell badly from the roof of an old mansion at Mosman Bay when a rusty rainpipe came away from the wall. I crashed to the ground and broke an arm and a leg. The police were called and I was taken to the Mater Hospital at Crows Nest. Two detectives from North Sydney Police Station went back to check my parents' house for goods they believed I had stolen. Under my bed they found a pair of Zeiss binoculars and, in the backyard, in a cage I had built at the back of my father's chook house, they discovered a paradise rifle bird and a pair of African lovebirds.

A Chain of Flashing Images

My childhood is a mystery to me, I hardly remember it. A reply Bob Dylan made to a reporter when asked to explain his songs describes it well. Dylan replied: 'A chain of flashing images.' Coming from a man who is one of the serious reasons I write it seems appropriate; his songs were the first sparks of enlightenment in the spiritual darkness during terms of my imprisonment. I remember words speaking to other words in darkness, phrases from the Bible read in a stripe of light as thin as a pencil coming under the bottom of a cell door. Lines illuminated by a swaying beam, swinging a searching arc from stone turret to cell block and reflected back on to the alkaline-smelling grey slate floor. Words talking to each other without letting me in on the conversation.

Memories from happier moments of my boyhood are mixed with sunlight and water, throbbing waves of sound, cicadas in peppermint trees, the early morning atmosphere around the shores of Sydney Harbour. The first flashing image is of a garden—my father's—where every day after school I would have to stand for an hour or so watering the vegetables. It's strange to remember it as a chore; forty years later one of the pleasures in my life is to water my own garden. It sounds pat, too good to be true, such symmetry. Life stories are a bit like that. It's when you want to innovate with language, to craft the words and

12

to use imagination that the trouble starts. These days poets find it difficult to respond to what goes on in their lives; the poet's material, language, has been questioned so thoroughly it seems almost folly to build with it. You have to think twice even before you begin.

Language theory is used by some of the French writers, like Maurice Blanchot who says *la negation est liée au langage*— a word is the memorial to what it signifies. Death is implicit in the distinction between sign and self. Cut away the dead wood until there is a risk in using a plane, let alone a chisel. Many writers feel that the horror of living in this age cannot be described, that poetry is no longer capable of speaking with any authority. All we can do is write an endless elegy in words that cannot convey the meaning of what they signify. All this is not so new, though it seems to be surfacing even in book reviews; I cannot write a book about my 'life' and make it interesting to any reader if I simply describe memories. I have been reading the work of the French poet Mallarmé for fifteen years now, and I do not pretend to understand it all, although it continues to fascinate. After some engagement with Mallarmé's texts, the notion of an elegy without words is making some sense to me.

The trouble with language theory is that poetry doesn't come from it. Writing is a craft a poet can learn; but without the ability to handle words like raw material a poet doesn't get very far. I was fortunate to grow up around people who were practising their craft and art.

The spirit of place is another thing a writer needs to understand. I grew up at Neutral Bay and on the Hawkesbury River. My mother's family were harbour people, my mother's mother a Scot and her husband a carpenter. My father's family were river folk, my father's mother was Irish and her husband was a lamp lighter and a fisherman. Both my grandmothers knew about folk song and poetry. My father loved horses and was also a fine gardener. I spent hours in my grandfather's workshop; his tools were kept meticulously in their places: his beautiful sharp planes and files; strange things like rasps; the fine chisels made in Scotland, honed daily on a wonderful oil stone in a cedar case; the measuring instruments; the levels with green eyes; and tapes that would stretch out from a round oval of brass then spring back like flat metal tapeworms. I understood the meaning of the word 'craftmanship' from both grandfathers. There was a craft in everything they did, one carving and planing wood, one weaving and binding nets and intricate crab hoops and snares. The odours follow me through the years: there was the French polish made from mixing turpentine, linseed oil and the crushed wings of a special African beetle, the sanding back, the emery paper wet and dry, the staining of rare wood. Then, on the Hawkesbury, the tanning of nets, the smell of a selection of gum barks and boiling the tannin, the permeating smell of tar from the oyster racks. It makes sense that I was drawn to the craft of using words, language, metaphors, images and phrasing them, polishing and bending, putting them together . . . the silver strophe . . . the canto bright with myth . . .

Prawns from Jerusalem

THE year I turned ten my grandfather let me work with him on his trawler during my school holidays. I felt very privileged about this because everybody knew that Fa-Fa preferred to work alone. His trawler was an old wooden boat with a diesel motor, and it was held together by green paint and his will. Painted on one side was the name *Dark Star*, and on the other was *Sissy*, the name of my grandmother. We all called it *Sissy's Star*. It was a prawn trawler, but Fa-Fa used it as a fishing boat. He stored his catch and slept on board and towed his net boats behind the stern. I loved being on board as it chugged up and down the river—I'd curl up in the cabin and half sleep, it felt like being in the chamber of a big green heart as the engine slowly pumped away and I breathed in salty fumes of diesel, oil and the pungent odour of jewfish.

We left his wobbly old jetty before dawn; it had been raining heavily for days and the river had turned an orange colour. It was a good time to fish downstream. In the bay between Juno Point and Eleanor Bluffs the river water hits the ocean tide, and this is where the big jewfish lurked, snatching mullet washed down in the flood. The water was so dark they fed as if it were night. We were going to fish here, but first we had to catch live bait. Fa-Fa knew the bait grounds in Cowan Creek, and the water in places like Jerusalem Bay was clear, washed by powerful tides and time spent lying in the deep valley.

It was just dawn and a fine mist hung above the surface of the bay, wisps curled around our green stern. I looked into the water, where big mushroom-shaped jellyfish floated by like parachutes in an upside down sky. Fa-Fa called them Portuguese Man-o'-wars; I looked again at them, reddish galleons adrift in the tide. We chugged up into the bay and over to the sandflats, the mist clearing as we cut the motor. Fa-Fa pulled in the net boat and we climbed on, while whipbirds cracked and their calls ricocheted from huge slabs of sandstone. We rowed slowly towards the shore, where the yellowtail would be starting to feed, then we both saw a man float up, one hand cutting the surface like a small pink fin. All he had on was a T-shirt and a pair of shorts. Something was wrong: I noticed the unnatural stiffness of his body. This was a dead man, and it was the first time I had seen a dead body. Fa-Fa checked my response; I looked to him for what to do next, but he was calm and told me, yes, he is dead, an oyster farmer or fisherman. He seemed to know there had been no foul play—he said 'drowned' in a tone of acceptance. He pulled our skiff over to the body, then touched it. It moved slowly like a waterlogged stump. The water was shallow and the sun was not yet warm; I watched carefully, but there didn't seem to be any smell. I wondered how long he had been here. Fa-Fa held up the jutting arm and the body rolled towards us, almost touching the bottom. Fa-Fa jumped out

17

and carefully turned the body a bit more, saying calmly 'Look.' Underneath, hundreds of prawns had gathered, hundreds, all clinging, feeding and swarming. The water was coloured by their translucent mass, a green shadow. He said 'the net', pointing to a prawn landing net in the belly of our skiff next to a gaff hook. I handed it over to him. He then started scooping under the body, catching dozens of prawns in each scoop. He pointed, gestured, to the fish boxes in the stern. I pulled them apart and lined them up. Fa-Fa went about the grim job, slowly, carefully, without words, scooping and turning the handle, filling the boxes. The prawns jumped in the boxes until their own weight sorted them out, then lay in layers finally with only the top flicking. The odd prawn jumped back into the belly of the boat, another out back into the water, while Fa-Fa scooped and carefully turned, scooped and turned. He treated the body with a stern respect, similar to the respect I have seen in his arms and hands when handling a big jewfish, holding the ninety-pound creature gently in his arms so as not to bruise the flesh, with a care not to damage the look of the beautiful shining kill. He handled those rare old fish like babies, packing them in ice, patting the golden flanks, staring down at them with reverence. He moved about this corpse with the same respect, took the same fierce care. Now came a test. Fa-Fa looked to the trawler anchored a hundred yards out in the bay. The net boat was sitting low in the water, its boxes full, the prawns shuddering down into themselves.

I started to get out, he said no, pass an oar. I handed it over and he plunged it into the sandy mud like a post, feeling that it was secure. He took twine, net cord he had woven by hand, I passed it in coils, and he tied it around the body. The body was now anchored. The smell was about, and I suddenly vomited. Fa-Fa looked into my eyes, put a strong arm over my shoulders and hugged me. I nodded. We rowed back, slowed down by the weight of the prawns. When we reached the side of the trawler, each box was hauled up by an old winch and swung onto the deck. Four heavy boxes—a day's work.

The Tobacco Tin Jewel Box

In winter on the river, July, August, when it was blowing a gale and raining, the fishermen would sit at the bar in The Angler's Rest and look out at the trees bending on the mountain behind The Gut. Old Dutch, Dutch Kerslake's dad, Old Moose, Phil (the Dill) Handy, Basil (Bigfoot), and old Fa-Fa, my grandfather—they'd sit around drinking beers with rum chasers, old beer or black and tan, they'd tell stories and complain about the weather. Back in those days, the money paid by the co-op for a big jewfish, a seventy to eighty pounder, could feed a family for two weeks. Catches of these great fish weren't rare, but they didn't happen on any regular basis. A month could pass between catches; other times, there'd be four or five caught in a month. Jewfish are beautiful-looking creatures: long, silver–gold flanks, a great bat tail, and their heads look so noble. They are the kings of the river. After World War II the fisheries officially renamed them mulloway and they are sold under that name in fish shops and at the markets, but the fishermen still just call them jews or jewies. They say the first name for them was jewel fish, because if you split the head apart in behind their eyes, like a third eye, is a little pearl-like bone that sits in a gland in front of the brain. Mulloway sometimes grow to seven feet in length and can weigh up to around a hundred and fifty pounds. Usually, the big ones are between sixty to ninety pounds. The bigger the fish the larger the 'jewel', and these jewels are beautiful things, like a real pearl: irregular, round and sometimes tear-shaped, they shine with an opalescent glow in sunlight. The jewels aren't worth taking out unless the fish is at least fifty pounds.

In the winter as it blew a gale the old codgers remembered the great fish in their lives and discussed the ways they had been caught. All the top men carried old tobacco tins—Golden Flake, Woodbine—and these tins had beautiful designs painted on the lids. Each fisherman had his tin and some carried them around for years; some had been handed down by their fathers. Inside these tins they carried their 'jewels'. When a drunken discussion started to go on the turn, before blows were thrown, some old bloke would just reach into his coat and take out the tin, with a movement resembling some strange ritual, the arm stretched out and the old, gnarled, black-freckled hand placed a tin on the bar. Then the old codger would say in a loud voice as he thumped the bar: 'Right!' Then things were sorted out, whose fish was bigger, in the winter of '42 or whatever. Old Dutch or Fa-Fa, out came all the tobacco tins, silence.

What a wonderful picture, these old gentlemen of the river, all opening their lids and carefully holding their 'jewels' in their sometimes very trembling hands. They placed them on the bar, then the fellow with the largest jewel would put it back in the tin and break the silence by rattling it in front of himself, shaking it like a gambler shakes his dice, mumbling his song of pride, gubba, gubba,

21

gubba . . . Then the barman would start pulling beers. They all had to buy the winner a middy a man. Ten or so beers would stand before him. Old Fa-Fa would chuckle and lick his lips—the night was his.

Mandy and the Firetails

I like to think that the first time I met Mandy was in the Brooklyn Cemetery. She has told me this isn't right; she says we first met playing out behind the fishermen's co-op. We'd go there to pinch ice from the wall of ice, a machine that built up a sheet of ice and then shattered it into thousands of thick flakes, ice the fishermen used to keep the catch fresh. Maybe she saw me there, but the first time we ever spoke was in the cemetery. In those days I wasn't supposed to be talking to her and none of my friends were either, including Dutch. Whenever he was told not to do something he felt compelled to do it, so he would just curse Mandy for the heck of it. She was a strange-looking girl, a bit of a tomboy except for her hair. She wore it in a ponytail, but it would fall apart and spill out over her shoulders—beautiful pure white hair, it was incredibly striking and grew in long waves. I don't know why we were told to keep away from her—something to do with her mother. There was gossip, whenever we were in the park or at some kind of function in town; you heard them, the other mothers, like a flat tune that would hum along any line they ever formed, waiting for the bus, at the shop. Mandy's mother didn't seem to give a stuff; she had a couple of mates, cousins maybe, and they'd drink together in her backyard. Instead of the pub on Saturdays they would put out a table in the yard and

23

sit around playing a radio, drinking and smoking and betting on the races. The gossip was a particularly vicious little song considering we didn't even know what Mandy's mum had done. They lived alone and her father was never mentioned. It was only after what happened in the graveyard that I looked back and realised I had been avoiding Mandy along with the others. Maybe Mandy likes to think we were friends all along because it must be painful to think of being so avoided.

The cemetery is the first thing you see, if you're looking, when you turn into Brooklyn Road from the Pacific Highway. It could be easily passed by if not for the wreath on the pole. Every few weeks an elaborate wreath of blood-red roses appears on the telegraph pole on the corner of the road, hung on a hook that has been hammered into the pole at about eye level. You can't miss it if it is still fresh, but after a few days the roses die and then it gradually turns into a circle of wire and the dead roses flap like old black rags in any stiff westerly. Then after a week or so it reappears, a new wreath, always the same blood-red roses entwined with ivy and leaves. Apart from the mysterious wreath it's easy not to notice the cemetery— it is sort of surrounded by a fence of scrubby brush. The day we met the wreath was on its last legs, just a tattered hoop of dead stalks.

I was in there trapping Indian myna birds. I had a vendetta against them because they were taking over the bush from native birds, like the finches, the double bars, the zebras, fairy wrens, jenny wrens, willy wagtails and the firetail finches. The mynas are introduced birds, parasites, and they lay their eggs in the nests of native birds; the eggs hatch and you can see tiny jenny wrens trying to feed these big, lousy myna birds. Oriental cuckoos do the same thing, but I don't have it in for them like I do for the mynas. In those days I was obsessed with birds; I wanted to be an ornithologist, but the problem was I couldn't spell and was hopeless at school with maths. I wouldn't have been able to spell ornithologist, yet I wanted to be one. I thought I'd skip school and get a job at Taronga Zoo cleaning bird cages, feeding and watering, work my way up by first-hand experience. I inquired and discovered I even needed a school certificate just to work in the cages. I dreamt I was writing a bird book, like Neville W. Cayley's *What Bird Is That?* Although I knew little about him at the time, Cayley was my hero and his book was the first book I owned. The only other books I remember being around at home were *Love Songs* by Robbie Burns, the Bible and a volume of the New South Wales Fisheries and Oyster Farms Act, 1935. It was bluntly called 'Regulations'. I was studying pigeons and had some road peckers I was training to home. My grandfather had homing pigeons and always kept one on his trawler, in the days before refrigeration. When he was right up the river and had a good haul he'd let the bird fly from his boat, and when it arrived home my grandmother would know to order more ice for the fish. One of my pigeons became a pet—a henbird I called

Bluey because she was a blue bar. One day she was torn from the sky and killed by a sea-eagle; falcons and hawks are always the 'enemy' to pigeon fanciers, but they weren't to me. The thing about Bluey's death was that although it nearly broke my heart I didn't feel any hate towards the eagle. There's still a glimmer of some weird kind of guilt hovering in the memory of Bluey when I see a harrier or eagle swoop down from the Hawkesbury sky and snatch up some fish or small bird. I notice the elegant circle and dive, the savage beauty in the way they kill.

Thinking back to the mynas and the Oriental cuckoos, I see the reason I didn't have it in for the cuckoo was that the fishermen called them 'prawnbirds'; every year their arrival signifies the beginning of the prawning season. With their long, monotonous, two-note call the birds drive everyone crazy because they sing just before dawn and the two notes go right through the brain of anybody anywhere near them. The prawns, however, cheer the fishermen up; at this time of the year they rise up from under the mud at the bottom of the river and on the dark of the moon they 'run'. The prawns swim in long thick schools and are scooped up by the prawners with seine nets, and the families live well again after the lean winter months.

I was in the graveyard trapping mynas with a couple of my grandfather's crab snares. I was concentrating— putting mullet gut in the traps for bait, pulling the long horse hair nooses free. Mandy came up behind me and gave me such a shock I jumped back and yelled. I was embarrassed at being caught off-guard, and when I recognised her I was even more surprised. I was fascinated with her: the town gossip made her even more interesting so I spoke to her. She asked me what I was doing. Usually whenever I tried to explain anything about birds to the other kids they'd lose interest after five minutes, but Mandy liked what I was saying and asked me to show her how to catch the mynas. We set the snares and caught a couple of birds.

I had a little cane creel with me to keep the caught birds in. I held one and carefully spread its wings to show her the lice crawling under the down, and I showed her the incredible orange-coloured throat and inspected its dirty beak. We put the bird into the creel and set more snares, then we moved back and wandered through the graves. I asked her if she knew where her father's headstone was and she silently led me to his grave. It was a plain slab of sandstone and it read: HARRY KERSLAKE, 1919–1960. That was it. Nothing about anyone remembering him, no mention of Mandy or her mother. I thought it was sad, and asked her if she came to look at it often. She said she'd only seen it once before. She hadn't even worked out how old he was when he died. I figured it out and said he was only forty. Yeah, forty, she said. I asked her how come he had died so young, what had happened? He just dropped dead one day in the chook yard while feeding the chooks, and when her mother found his body it was covered in ants. She still didn't seem upset or sad. I asked her almost without talking, looking gently into her eyes, what she felt. Mum reckons we're better off without him, was all she said.

I changed the subject and we talked about birds again. I started by saying that I wondered what happened when a myna dropped dead: would the lice keep eating the blood when it went cold? If it was in a chook yard the chooks would probably peck out its eyes, I thought, and the ants would start on it then, they would eat the lice because lice were small and maybe more tender. Then again, maybe lice were hard like fleas; they are so small it's hard to tell. We talked on about all those kinds of things, totally involved in the secret invisible world of ants, lice and dead creatures.

Maybe we got a bit carried away, but we decided to do some experiments. We looked into the fishing creel and saw that one of the birds had bent its primary wing feathers, so that made the choice easier. I took out the poor bent-feathered bird, held it like my father had taught me and snapped its neck. We set the other one free, and it whirred away on its wings and skimmed the tops of the gravestones as it bobbed and dived for its freedom into the tick bush. We decided we'd put the other into a chook yard, leave it there for a day and then return to see what had happened.

We decided to take it to Moose's place, because he lived just down the road and his father had chooks and ducks in the yard. We were walking to the road when we heard a humming noise. Looking back to the bush where the sound was coming from we saw the most amazing sight. Suddenly, a whole clump of bushes went red, dark red. The colour moved like a wave down over the curve of the bush and back to the top. It changed again and the bush shook wildly, the colour now gone.

We started walking towards the bush, which was still shaking, when the wave of red reappeared, rippling up and down and turning from green to red. There was a chattering sound coming from the bush. We got closer and the bush exploded with hundreds of tiny firetail finches, hundreds of them in the one bush thick as leaves. I had never seen so many. They flew up and then back away up the hill in a great red flock, a disintegrating wave, scattering red flecks up the hillside. We ran after them, tearing through the tick bush and up over the huge broken boulders of sandstone. We made it halfway up the hill and then fell down in a clearing. Exhausted, we saw that we had come a long way up, and we could see a little waterfall and a creek. We both lay on the soft ground, which was covered in fallen leaves that rustled under our bodies. We were close and I looked over and Mandy looked back. I put my arms around her. We lay there for maybe ten minutes. I turned and kissed her softly. We kissed and hugged each other for a long time and finally we clumsily half undressed and made love. We stayed there until the sun started to go down, got up, smoothed our clothes and started walking down the hill together. We reached the cemetery and there we saw the creel with the dead bird inside it.

We walked to Moose's, put the bird in his chook yard with the ducks and then walked all the way back to Brooklyn, holding hands for the last half mile. Mandy was the first girl I ever thought of as being beautiful: her face was flushed and her hair was a bush of white silk. Her quick smile vanished almost as soon as it appeared, as if she felt smiling was something you shouldn't do. I left her at the edge of the railway crossing, where a steam train hissed and gurgled by with its wheels sparks on the first of the night's dark.

A Hawk, Dutch, and Flathead Creek

THE river was silk; my boat pushed through it, a steady triangle of wake at the stern. A swamp harrier flew alongside, just above the surface. Darting now and again it skimmed the river, kissing the run in. I felt great— swamp harriers were always a good sign, and fairly rare, and this one was my guide. When birds came near the boat I threw them a fish, some gut or head; different birds had their particular ways, ripping, guzzling, or diving. I didn't throw anything to the hawk—it wasn't after dead fish, it was dreaming of prey.

I was trying to get to the top of the creek before dark. Dutch had left our moorings at The Gut around midday, so had three hours on me. We thought that by stringing our nets together we'd be able to net off the whole top part of the creek, around two hundred yards. It's called a creek, though it's really an arm of the estuary; there's a waterfall at the top that sprinkles down great slabs of sandstone into a mangrove swamp. The tide was running up, so if we had our nets out on the high we'd trap every fish in the creek. Flathead was 'closed waters', so we'd have to be careful in case Fisheries' inspectors or wardens from the Parks and Wildlife happened to be around. Dutch would be up there now, checking it out, getting the feel, looking for buried snags and deciding where to shoot the nets.

As the river narrowed I could see The Wreck coming

up on my right. An hour and I'd be there. The net was lying in perfect loops and coils, ready to shoot. The boat was clean and dry and everything was in place. The fish boxes were stacked and I had plenty of ice. The swamp harrier, still with me, swooped and darted alongside. I was thinking ahead, wondering if we'd pull off the plan and not get caught.

I knew I could depend on Dutch: he was pretty crazy, but he knew the river as well as anyone. His family were all river rats, three generations of them. The thing with Dutch was that although he was wild when he wasn't on the river, he could be a different person and he was incredibly shy with women. He would drink at The Angler's Rest with the other fishermen, then every time a girl came into the bar, he'd start, go into his act. Hava look at her, she's the one, I'm gunna get her, like tonight man. Then he'd sit back and get totally drunk. Or he'd sit there saying all these things until the girl left and then he'd leave and follow after her. Then the next day he'd turn up at the co-op and tell us what a great night he'd had and how fantastic the girl had been. Maybe Dutch wasn't all that great with the girls, but with the fish he was a killer. He'd tell me that he knew the way fish thought because he'd been a fish in another life. I said, wouldn't that make it harder for him to catch them? Oh no, mate, it's such a fucked life swimming around in the drink eating mud and prawns all the time they are happy to be put out of their misery.

As I turned the bend into Flathead Creek I could see him sloshing in the black mud. He was wading through the mud with marsh flies and sandflies clinging to him and sucking the sweat that was pouring from the top half of his body. Dutch carried a great club, a half-branch of mangrove; he swung and hammered it, breaking up the oysters growing on the shore rocks. Aaah, aaarrr, yaaaaraha! he went as he carried out his fierce havoc. The rich Hawkesbury mud squelched about him. A heron kept its distance behind him, picking flesh from the smashed shells. Breaking the oysters was a part of our plan: we'd been doing it every second day for a week. We knew it would attract fish, that they'd all start going up there to feed on the wrecked oysters. Whole schools of them: bream, flathead, jewies, mullet, whiting—every type of fish in the river. Then, by netting the creek off at high tide, we'd have them.

I was almost on top of Dutch before he saw me, my boat skidding on a mudbank. Dutch looked up, haayee, yeaaha! We made our hunting calls, kings of the swamp, the catch already rocking in the bellies of our boats. The tide was high, the last of the sun was about to drop behind the mountain above the creek, and fish were making circles on the tight water running under us.

We set the nets, and the night popped with the sound of fish slapping and struggling to their ends with wounded gills snared in the mesh. We were crouched on the bank, smoking, watching the corkline writhing just under the surface like some kind of sea serpent a hundred yards long, burning and sparkling with phosphorescence. I was overwhelmed with strange feelings: night's blood was shooting through my brain, the tide was running out, the Hawkesbury night, the fish were sounding their death struggles, nets, mangroves, stars, and the hooting laughter of a nightjar.

Then the night came exploding into the boat, everything went crazy, and Dutch howled among the fish, rocking the boat. A great thumping came on the surface a few yards off the stern. I thought it was some huge stingray, lifting one of its wings and dropping it. Next thing, whaacckkk! It was a big jewfish, its jaw breaking down on the surface like a rabbit trap. Water bulged and the old bull fish cut loose, its tail lashing down and splattering us with mud and spray. It rose up to its full length, a silver trunk in the moonlight, then it crashed down and stampeded into the net. The stern swung around and the net rope hissed, tearing through the night. The great fish rolled over and over, strangling itself in the fine deadly monofilament of the nylon mesh. We got the monster of a fish into the boat as dawn broke; it was as big as Dutch. We looked at each other and then at the fish lying down the centre of the boat.

The first sunlight burnt our faces. We looked about at the carnage: the whole creek was a mess of death. Our nets were twisted hopelessly, there were fish everywhere, the ice was melting, mud crabs were dragging themselves through the mesh, and there were dead stingrays and mullet floating belly up. Even a poor wood duck was caught and was flapping about. We released it and sat down on the fish boxes. We were covered in slime from jellyfish, and our hands stung with fine cuts. The whole creek was calm, silent. By now the birds would normally be fluting and singing in the mangroves, but not even a kingfisher looked out from the branches. We looked at each other for a long moment, knowing we would never be able to fish Flathead Creek again.

YOU ARE MY SUNSHINE

My vision reeked of the truth.

VLADIMIR NABOKOV

◆

Teen Angel

THE narrow dirt road lined with poplars and neat hedges led to a square of asphalt. The assembly ground of Mount Penang was surrounded by long weatherboard huts, which were dormitories with wire grid windows. Behind them another road led to the lawns and gardens in front of the officers' houses. Here in the mornings you'd find boys washing cars, mowing the lawns, or weeding the gardens along the drives. Inside the houses houseboys would be making the beds of their keepers or doing the breakfast washing up. Cleaning shoes or polishing silver were jobs the other boys coveted, but these jobs were for the privileged boys who had behaved themselves and would be weeks or months away from their eighteenth birthdays and release. The inmates here were all between ten and eighteen years of age, juvenile offenders and wards of the state.

The youngest boys were ten year olds with translucent faces. They worked in the mess with wax rags and sandsoap, their bodies sweating under grubby white smocks. Their undiscovered bodies drifted over the hardwood floors, their dark string fringes wet or their blond curls limp in the sweet-smelling atmosphere. They had dirty fingernails, front teeth out, their noses were runny and they had oyster-shell smiles and lips with cold sores. Chilblains ate into their fingers and toes. The sweet-faced vicious young boys of the Officers' Mess were ever-changing virgins, their needs as lucid as the yellowbox honey they poured over the porridge. They fought behind the boilers with fists and arms, their teeth, or with feet up against hot metal, or with broken glass or forks in their hands or fence wire staples between their fingers. The terror of sex was hidden in the back of their minds as they wiped cum from their fingers in fear of discovery and ridicule.

Looking down from the quarterdeck on to the sports-ground you could see spur-winged plovers bob along in the stormwater drain, their creaking calls echoing over the football field. Some mornings rainbow lorikeets swooped through the mist in the coral trees and landed outside the ablution block, where old Flophead the school teacher stood, smoking and spitting into the fog before muster.

The red road was an artery we marched along on Saturday mornings; it led to the dam where we swam in water so cold you'd get cramps in your eyes. It was worse when we climbed out to an order to stand to attention in the August wind, until the screw would give the next order to pick up your towel. Then there was the march back and punishment if you spoke or fell out with a stone in your boot or if a lace came loose. We marched around the assembly ground for hours in the cold with our noses running and pains shooting through our heads like burning wire. We marched around and never got it right and were never ordered to stop until we did, until we marched and then were so right the other boys started to hate us.

Work days were spent digging rock-hard earth, building a road that went nowhere, straight out through the bush, on the top of a mountain in the middle of nowhere. This crazy road led no place and just wrecked the bush. We knew it was meant that way to make us feel even more useless than we already felt, with picks and spades and a sledge-hammer cracking the callouses on our filthy hands until they'd bleed. Then the implement would slip through the blood and cut your foot bad, but not bad enough to stop, and the sun made you sick and yet you couldn't faint. If you did you'd lose points or be thrown into the Black Peter next to Blond Barry, who was always in there, his remission gone, his hair cut off and his voice hissing through the tongue he'd sliced with a razor. Blond Barry who would piss bright orange piss and eat dirt or swallow lighted cigarettes. Your turn would be next.

If you were under fifteen it would be the school room with old Flophead. He knew we had never been to proper schools and couldn't write much, so he would get us to write compositions and then read them back to the class. He would ask what kind of existence had led to this tragic spectacle; holding a page of somebody's writing between his finger and thumb he'd wave it about and say it was gibberish and too painful for him to behold. He would then try to introduce us to some culture by making us listen to a radio programme called the 'John Dease Hit

Parade of Popular Classics'. He'd close the blinds and say it was so we could 'concentrate', but it was so he could have a slug of his flask of whisky. His breath was as sour as the yard behind the school house where the swine were wallowing in the slops.

Flophead was better than the other screws, though he did his time easy in the warm school room, which was a paradise compared to the working party out there digging their meaningless road through the rock-hard red dirt of the mountain. On the verandahs around the dorms there were special work groups, which were made up of kids who were queer, mentally retarded or Aboriginal. The Koorie boys were always so much better at this work, which was darning socks—they would darn over the holes in stitches so beautifully woven they looked better than the original cloth. They kept to themselves and could still darn in the winter with frostbite eating into their fingers. The others looked down on the verandah boys, but really they had a more comfortable existence than any of us.

On the verandah of the building they called the quarter-deck there was always some boy doing punishment—this was called 'holy-stoning the deck'. The boy would have to get down on his hands and knees and rub a whitestone brick back and forth for hours on end. This activity, over time, had worn a groove two-foot wide in the hardwood, because it was always the same spot, back and forth, back and forth until you felt as if a stream of molten lead was pulsing up and down your spine. Blisters would form on top of blisters on your knees, the water would break and your shins would bleed and sting and burn until you were crying. Now and then one of these boys would crack up and jump the deck and run. The officers called this 'going dingo', and if it happened the privileged boys would be called out to chase after the kid. You would hear somebody yell dingo! dingo! and the cry would be taken up into a chorus of a cruel, taunting chant. The boys were just like human bloodhounds running the poor kid to ground, then they would grab him and rip into him, tearing his clothes and grabbing his balls and twisting. It would be hell for the kid until the screw finally ambled up, looked down, and said, 'Okay, cuff him. I'll deal with the little mongrel now.' They'd throw him into the Black Peter and feed him on bread and water for a week.

In the dormitory the beds were in long rows, only inches apart. Clothing was sprinkled with water and placed under the mattress—the weight of the boy was meant to press the clothes. So at night they would sit there hunched up on a little square of hard wood, then they'd place their little bundles of pressed clothes at the foot of their bed and wait until the screw came around and checked, giving each boy 'points'. These points would be added up at the end of each week and the boys would be moved a section higher or a section lower; the lower the section the less privileges. You'd lose points for small things like talking softly after lights out. On Friday nights there was a sad version of 'talent time'. Boys could stand by their beds

43

and sing a song, and they were judged by counting hands. Only a few boys had the courage to do it, and then usually they were terrible. A young Aboriginal boy whose name was Joe Monday always won. He only performed one or two songs: 'The Royal Telephone' and 'Teen Angel'. When he sang 'Teen Angel' he would almost break our hearts—it was like church if you still believed in God. I can't imagine ever hearing another voice as pure; Joe Monday sang the lyrics as if he had written them and his voice was the most tender sound ever to fill the great empty cavern of that weatherboard prison. 'Are you somewhere up above and are you still my own true love . . .' Then the lights would go out, the boys would rustle into their beds, the screw would throw the switch of the security alarm and then speak into a microphone, his metallic voice saying, 'No boy to be relieved without permission and no talking after lights out . . .'

Skin Deep

WE were marching, out of step and heel kicking. It was very hot, our shirts clung to our backs and our boots rubbed our ankle skin raw. We marched up over a cobbled road made of sandstone, out into a paddock of red dirt. We passed a few trees, grim-looking scribbly gums scorched by recent scrub fire. The odd crow would land in one of the trees, shaking branches and crowing the most horrible song it knew, wooorrrk, wwooorrrkk, work, as ash like huge flakes of dandruff came floating down onto our faces. A small branch gave up and fell, thunk. We marched, incapable of remembering or inventing crow jokes. We marched harder, only to crumble clumps of clay that fell into our boots under sweat-drenched socks.

After another hour the screw called Company Halt. There we stood, in the middle of a barren paddock, sixty sun-frazzled delinquents doing it hard. We had to dig, in three rows; you'd do one spadeful, in, out, then move one pace left. When you reached the end of the line you would have to walk back around behind the row you were in and then start digging at the other end. This was the only time you could look up, and it would give your aching back a bit of a rest. I'd look out, hoping to see some birds. Sometimes the digging would attract willy wagtails, or maybe double bar finches or even firetails searching for seeds in the mounds of uprooted wild grass.

It looked by the sun to be around ten o'clock—two hours until our lunch break. The sun was doing my neck harm, burning even behind my ears; we were not allowed to remove our sweaty shirts, probably the only order we were ever given that made some kind of cruel sense. I'd had enough—nothing could be more terrible than this—so I thought I'd make a break. There was a valley at the end of the paddock that looked a hundred times closer than it was by now, and I was a good runner; the only sport I had ever been able to do, in fact, was marathon running. My heart thumped like a little tom-tom drum and fear trembled through my gut.

I was digging next to a kid named Beale, who was pushing up against the side of my leg and dropping his shovel down where I was about to plant mine. My spade would hit his and I'd jar my arm; it was one of the oldest tricks of torment in the book and the dumbest. I was getting sick of Beale, so I told him to cut it. He just gave me this big stupid grin and pushed me further. Beale didn't know me—he must have thought I'd just keep copping his mindless aggravation. I guess I didn't really look like I would put up much resistance. Beale wasn't all that big, but he did look incredibly mean. I knew nothing short of violence, some kind of a brawl, would stop him. It was what I needed for an excuse.

Beale had managed to draw in everything around me; my temper flashed and shorted out somewhere between my temples. Beale drew it all in, the random hate, the mechanical soul-destroying digging, the irritating red dirt. The entire paddock became a theatre of meaningless hurt. Black trees climbed up out of the ground, cows moaned across the grim scrub, heat waves curved down from the sun. The screw stood over us, a swaying tower of fat calling up tools, down tools, move it fools. All of it looked the same dead-coloured red dirt. It coloured my brain when I closed my eyes and my spade hit aimlessly down into this red, dead earth.

Beale moved his spade across, twisting it into my shin. I crouched down with the pain, my shovel held tightly with both hands, strangling the dead grey wooden handle. The digging row of boys fluttered, shovels out of step. I pulled myself up and around in one move; I came face to face with Beale. The blade of my tool was now a weapon, and it shot up and crunched in under his jaw, cutting deep into the flesh and bone without me even consciously taking aim. Beale's mouth became a gash of red, and I moved back. He came roaring forward, a crazed upright beast, his spade shooting out into the faces, heads and arms of the boys around him. The screw came wailing through the midst of it all. The blood of boys seeped into the colour of that dug paddock.

You Are My Sunshine

BLOND Barry often sat in the boiler room. Outside on the parade ground it was winter, but in the boiler room steam, dank mould, coke smoke and the furnace itself created an atmospheric brew resembling summer. Blond Barry wasn't exactly in charge of the boiler room; it wasn't his official job, he just made it his domain. Nobody disputed this: screws, the social worker, not even The Gash, the hospital matron. Cheezy Borgese, the Deputy Superintendent of Mount Penang Training School for Boys, usually ran the ablution block and he would turn a blind eye—all he checked was the amount of coal consumed. Cheezy was the officer we all loved to hate; he had a mean streak, though his main weapon was his fearful-sounding voice. It frightened the shit out of the new boys and the rest of us learnt to keep out of his way.

The boiler room was the most exotic place in the boys' home. On its walls were posters, clippings and photographs cut from magazines, images of our dreams, American cars—Mustangs, Thunderbirds, Cougars, Stingrays and Customlines. The packing-case shelves were stocked with tins and jars, coffee, tea and sugar. It was the place where the head boys did deals, made plans; it was the headquarters of our resistance fighters—our secret underground gambled there.

When Blond Barry wasn't locked up in the Black Peter he'd be there running the boiler room, sitting there for hours on end, sitting and watching the blue flames lick the coal until it was coke. Once in a while he'd stand and throw a lump of coal into the fire. We'd see him from behind, the fire glowing through his head of curls like a red halo. We were always a bit afraid of him, as he'd been inside longer than any of us and he said he couldn't even remember what it was like on the outside. Even Cheezy Borgese was edgy about Blond Barry and he gave him a wide berth, until Barry went too far. Like the time he came walking out onto the parade ground with no clothes on, except for his cowboy hat, his arms loaded up with burning coals. He strode straight through the muster; the whole of Two Company parted before him as he walked forward. He was singing at the top of his voice, the burning coal cradled in his arms leaving a great billowing trail of smoke and steam smelling of poached flesh behind him in the freezing air. It took six screws to hold him down, and the whole time Barry sang his heart out: 'You are my sunshine, my only sunshine, please don't take my sunshine away . . .' They couldn't put the straitjacket on him because the burns were too dreadful, so Barry had to be held down for an hour until he exhausted himself. Even pumped full of tranquillisers his energy frightened them.

Blond Barry would never explain his behaviour, which was the reason we could always believe in him. He was living proof to us that we were all still in there fighting, resisting, that the war wasn't over, our spirits could not be broken. So when Barry sat in the boiler room the tension would mount. Sometimes he would sit there for weeks, his presence becoming more and more potent. We'd wait until the coast was clear and duck in with our offerings: all forms of contraband, eggs from the fowl yards, milk from the cows, wood, balls of string, anything, things we thought he might fancy. But Blond Barry just sat there, unaware of most of our gifts, oblivious to everything but the warmth.

SEA OF HEARTBREAK

What about me, and my words? If I write or if I speak,
wouldn't it be as a form of dissimulation?
I am fully involved with myself, thoroughly
in conspiracy with the Shadow.

FRANCIS PONGE, 1924

◆

The Girl with the Black Velvet Band

I was seventeen years old, I lived at Neutral Bay, and it was 1959. I'd just taken possession of my first car—a Ford Mercury. It was a 1945 model and was a side-valve V8 with three months' rego. Three months—eternity. I bought it from Wanda, a girl who knocked around with some bikies from Crows Nest. She wanted two hundred quid and I'd given her half, saying I'd pay the rest in two weeks. It had taken a year to save the hundred, so there wasn't much chance of raising the rest in a fortnight. I didn't care; I had my first car, it was a Ford, a V8 and was shining black. I knew something would have to happen after the time ran out, because if I didn't come good with the money Wanda would send her bikie friends around to collect. After two weeks I'd have to work something out.

My parents wouldn't allow me to have a car, so I had to park it a few streets away from my place. I had no licence, and my learner's permit had been cancelled—cars were already a big problem in my life. In those days you could drive around without a licence if you didn't do something crazy, like drag-racing in French's Forest, or doing demos or wheelies outside the milkbar. If you drove carefully and didn't speed you could get away with it. In the 1950s the cops in Sydney had Holdens and we all knew a V8 Ford could leave them for dead, if you were

53

crazy and could drive well. These things were like hard facts. We didn't read much more than *Pix* or handbooks for Fords; I don't remember anyone reading a book back then, and I'd never heard of Jack Kerouac or his friend Neal Cassidy. We did know a kid, Ricky Kay, who was a crazy car-driving getaway hero like Dean Moriarty in *On the Road*, and Ricky Kay was real life while the poets and writers who wrote books didn't come into my life until I was twenty-four. I'll never know how things would have turned out if we had known about things like *On the Road*, *A Season in Hell*, and *Howl*; maybe things would have gotten even more out of control if I'd read them before my first couple of escapades—who knows? America seeped in through the jukebox and on the screens at the Southern Cross and the Orpheum. There wasn't much in the way of a spiritual life available in the 1950s at Neutral Bay; there was the harbour, the birds and animals and that was about it.

I worked as an apprentice for a Dutch pastry cook in his cake shop at Naremburn. I worked long hours, from dawn till dusk, and every day after work I'd drive straight to the local milkbar to show off my car. The milkbar was on the top of a suburban hill called Crows Nest, and all the kids would hang out there. We'd line our cars up on the street outside, then polish and admire them. Sometimes we'd sit there revving the motor, hoping the girls would look out. We'd go in and muck around playing snooker, and at times a floating poker game would appear. We'd stand around playing the jukebox, Don Gibson and Sam Cooke sang about love, lonesome number one, the sea of heartbreak; the jukebox played, our memories ticked away.

The same songs are still playing, the fashions circle back, songs turn dreams to reality, characters change, people die, the stories repeat. Those songs travelled with us in our cars, the myths colouring our sentiments—lost love and loneliness, how we longed for that sweet caress. Oh, so divine, on that sea, the sea of heartbreak. The songs were playing when I caught my first glimpse of Carol. I tried to catch her eye; I wanted to talk to her straight away, but it was too hard, I was shy, the other boys were chatting her up, I couldn't approach her. Sandy Stan was giving her coins for the jukebox and buying her Cokes. I asked my friend String what her name was. String knew everything, but not much about her. She had just turned up a few days ago, and nobody knew where she lived or where she came from. She had some kind of Irish accent. It was crazy—she was the centre of attention, so why would she be interested in me? She could have anyone she wanted, and she probably had a boyfriend anyway. I gave up—it was too difficult, too painful. I had to sleep.

The next morning I was driving down the road at 4 a.m., going to work. The streets were empty; it had been raining and the roads were shiny black ribbons. The motor idled as I coasted down Willoughby Road saving petrol. Next thing I saw two figures, two girls walking down the street as if it was daylight, one with a cloth bag and the other a beach towel. They looked so strange hitching a ride.

I swung the car over to the side and asked where they were going. They jumped straight in without even talking; I noticed one of them was very young, just a kid, and the other was, to my amazement, Carol. I asked again where they were going. 'We don't know.' 'What do ya mean you don't know?' Carol said: 'Well, we just have to go, the child welfare's after us because our mother shot through.' 'What do you mean, shot through?' Then Carol started telling me their story. They came from Ireland—they had arrived in Australia, and their father was some kind of a seaman. They had been here six months, then a month after they got here their father had pissed off and their mother had started bringing blokes home every night, drunk. Things got really bad, and they knew their mother didn't even want them—she sounded like a nightmare. They hadn't been to school, and they were being thrown out of their flat. Then, a few nights ago, their mother hadn't come home. They had been living on baked beans, milk and the hamburgers Carol had been scoring at the milkbar. The other people in the flats where they lived noticed the mother's absence and had called welfare. They had nothing; Carol had been going to the milkbar before her mother had left and just continued to get the boys to buy her hamburgers and stuff so she could save some for her sister.

I couldn't really take it all in, take any of it in, though

I was impressed thinking of her going through this daily masquerade, fixing her hair, putting on the make-up, getting dressed up and going out while her sister waited, starving, at the flat. I thought at first she was exaggerating, that she was making it up, then I thought: what did it matter, if she wanted me to believe all this it was bad enough, things were out of control. Even if she had made some of it up there still had to be some dreadful truth to it all. Nobody would make up a story like this if something wasn't drastically wrong. I was trying to take it all in, thinking at the same time of the contradiction—here she was, yesterday my dream girl, the one I thought I'd never even get to speak to, and now here she was, stranded, an orphan, wanting my help. Her sister was only a little girl of nine. What was happening? It felt unreal, yet there wasn't anything more real than these two girls sitting there in my car. I said: 'Okay, listen. Here's what we'll do— you stay in the car, and I'll park out the back of my work. Wait and I'll get you something to eat—it might take a while until my boss has a break. Just wait, and whatever happens I'll think of something.'

I parked the car, left them in it and went into the cake shop. I started making all these things for the morning, and all this stuff for lunch. Pies, teacakes, cream buns, finger buns, cream horns, cream puffs—all the usual pastries and cakes. I was making sausage rolls, spreading huge sheets of pastry over the workbench and piping out long lines of mince meat mixed with breadcrumbs, rolling them up, painting them with egg and milk, cutting them into the right sizes and thinking of Carol. I was spinning out in my head, but my hands were doing all these normal things, ordinary things, ridiculous things. Would she still be out there, what was she thinking? Four hours went by, then Mr Van said: 'Okay, see you in an hour. Check the bread dough, see if it's proving—don't burn anything!'

As soon as he went out the front door I grabbed a box and started filling it with things: buns, pies, some fancy stuff, chocolate eclairs. I ran out to see if they were still there. They were, sitting up in the morning sun on the front seat of the Merc. I couldn't believe it. I gave them the stuff. 'Here, eat these, take it easy, don't do anything, just wait until I knock off.' Somehow I managed to work through the afternoon; I put Carol out of my mind, or tried to. I worked until six, then I ran out and they were still there—I was elated. I knew then and there that me and Carol were going to end up together, that somehow this would work out.

The night before this miracle had been a normal night: tea at home, the whole family around the kitchen table— my sister, myself, my two brothers and Mum and Dad. It had been Tuesday, and we'd had hot silverside with white sauce sprinkled with parsley, mashed potatoes with cabbage and carrots cut in circles, and rhubarb and custard for sweets. After the silent meal, before dessert, my mother had started one of her little lectures on good behaviour and manners; she talked on, addressing my sister although her words generally floated unnoticed through the air.

'There was this dreadful looking creature at the bus stop, this terrible girl, nasty piece of work I'm sure. Well, there at the bus stop in front of everyone, brazen—putting on make-up, plastering it on, and her clothes, well, they certainly weren't for school. No school would take her dressed like that, fishnet stocking things, at her age and a school day, just flaunting it. There was no intention of school in her mind—proper little hussy.'

I couldn't tell from what my mother was saying what this girl had actually done, other than existing in the same world as us. Well, everything about her was wrong and it could rub off, and my mother told my sister Jenny that if she ever turned out like that it would break her heart, break her mother's heart, it would probably kill her. Who'd ever marry someone like that? What kind of a man would marry a little floosy, what kind of horror did life hold in store for her? On she went, while I tried to imagine the girl; she certainly didn't sound like any of the local girls at Neutral Bay. Mum always noticed the smallest details, then blew them out of all proportion. Terrible things could be in store for us too if we strayed from her narrow path; I was immune to her prophesying. Dad mumbled about the garden never being watered right, and asked who it was that kept feeding his chook food to the bloody pigeons.

I drove away from work wondering what to do next and remembering my mother's strict attitude concerning the behaviour of young women. What on earth would she make of Carol and her sister? Carol wasn't like the girl she had been talking about at the table the night before. Well to me she wasn't—although I knew if I turned up with both Carol and her sister—that would be too much. As we cruised down Falcon Street, we had what seemed like a practical conversation. Where to go, how would we live, whether the Child Welfare people were hot on our trail? We skirted around these thundering inevitables. Things had taken such a turn for the better for Carol who seemed pleased with anything I suggested. My mind sailed ahead of the car as we burbled along through Neutral Bay. It didn't seem much of a problem. We just had to find a place to camp until we worked things out. I told Carol how happy I was to be talking to her. I told her how I had been admiring her from the other side of the milkbar, how I had started to fall in love with her. I talked on and on, saying all the things I thought I should say, like lines from songs. I ended up saying I was secretly in love with her. She didn't seem to mind, she seemed to like what I was saying. It was all so perfect, so effortless, unreal in a way like a dream. Then she was agreeing, she'd go with me. She thought I was alright, but what about Wendy, what about her sister, where was she going to stay? Who would look after her?

I was driving down towards the bay, down Karrabah

Road and we passed Mick Morgan's place. Mick lived in this huge old rambling house with his mother and brothers and sisters. The house was always full of kids. I didn't even know some of their names. Mick was one of my best friends. He didn't have a father. Mrs Morgan was a kind woman who understood us more than any of the other mothers. I don't know how she got by, but there was always food in the place and Mick's friends were always welcome. Some of the back rooms were inhabited by mysterious 'lodgers' and we had to keep out of their way.

We stopped the car and went in. Mick was there and he couldn't believe it—me just walking in with Carol like that. Mick was one of the boys who had actually got to know her a bit. I knew he was keen on her as well. I asked him about the chances of Carol's sister staying awhile and he asked his mother. Carol told Mrs Morgan the story about her father shooting through. She told the whole story, everything, about her mother leaving, the Child Welfare— only this time she really laid it on thick. Mrs Morgan was moved. I could tell she was impressed with Carol. She said Wendy could stay until things were sorted out, and I told her I was going to take Carol home to my place. She said it was alright by her, she had it in for the welfare: 'Child Welfare', she said, 'what bloody welfare—I wouldn't let those bastards near a dog. Welfare what a joke.' She said Wendy would be a cousin visiting them from Ireland with her auntie. We said we'd be back and finally said goodbye and left. We got back into the car and drove off. It all seemed so simple.

We arrived at my place and walked straight in. My mum was in the kitchen cooking tea. I said I've got my girlfriend with me. She said that's nice or something without looking up. I suppose she thought I was with Bev. I had broken up with Bev a few weeks before and I hadn't said anything about it to my mother. I said: 'Mum, this is Carol. You haven't met. Can she stay here, she's got nowhere to go?'

My mother looked up from her cooking and almost had a heart-attack—she just stared at me and Carol. Carol was the girl she had seen at the bus stop, the girl who was the absolute epitome of everything my mother disapproved. She looked at me with a cold blue glare, a gaze that might kill, then she slowly turned and walked out of the kitchen, silence crackling in her wake. This all happened in seconds but I felt it would go on forever. I couldn't believe what was happening: here was Carol, the girl I had been waiting to meet for years, the most incredible girl I had ever spoken to. Maybe she was a bit wild but she was beautiful—to my mother, though, she was a harlot from Babylon.

Thinking back on it all it seems pathetic. How could this meeting, this small incident, how could it have had such an outcome. How could Carol have been such a threat to my mother—she was just a lost girl really, a deserted child.

I followed mum into the living room and before I could

say anything she said: 'Get her out of here. Your father will be home in a few minutes, if she's not out of here by then all hell will break loose.' I said that if she had to leave then I would be leaving with her and wouldn't be back. She would have said something along the lines of: 'This is the way we live, and if you can't live by our rules, if you can't live like us then go and live by your own rules and don't blame me for what happens.' She always said things like: 'You have to take the bad with the good, you like it or lump it, enough is enough, I'm not impressed . . .' all those dreadful old sayings you hear people say, but she meant them. I can still hear her twisting those terrible platitudes into reality: 'Well you made the bed so you lie in it, you reap what you sow . . .' What she said would happen was going to happen—there was no way of talking about it, I could take it or leave it. So we went.

I held Carol's hand and we walked around the block and got into the car. Carol wasn't fazed by it, she took it for granted. She was used to much worse. We drove up to the milkbar and I bought a couple of hamburgers and a bottle of Coke and then I drove down to Primrose Park and we sat in the car eating the hamburgers and looking out across the bay. The surface of the water was being flattened out by thin rain making thousands of tiny dimples. There was a breeze coming across the bay and it carried the smell of blackberries and the warm stink from the stormwater drains. I couldn't tell but Carol seemed to think everything was under control. What were we going to do? All I had was five quid and a tank of petrol. Where were we going to go? The next day was a workday for me, but going to work would mean I had to leave Carol alone for the fourteen hour shift at the cake shop—and besides, making chocolate eclairs and fairy fingers seemed to make as much sense as one of my mother's sayings.

We spent that first night together in a place Carol had discovered when she was running from the welfare, in a lane down the back of Crows Nest. It was an old stables full of hay and chaff bags and there was an old draught horse there who snorted throughout the night. We pulled up an old tarp and filled it up with straw, cuddled up and talked our way into the morning. I told Carol I loved her and wanted to spend the rest of my life with her. I told her stories about Queensland, stories I'd heard from other boys when I was in Gosford Boys Home, tales of pawpaws growing on the side of the roads, bananas every-where, fish in every river, warm nights and sun on the beaches. Carol's dream was for us to get a flat, for me to get a job in Queensland as a pastry cook, to set up the flat and then bring her sister up. I said we could live there, change our names and stay together until we were old enough to get married. It would all work out if we could make it across the border to Queensland; like in a movie, if we could make it across the border it would all work out.

We woke in the morning smelling of hay; there was

a sweet smell of horse shit in the air, and I knew somebody would be coming soon to tend to the horse. Our faces were all crinkled from being pressed into the pillows of straw, but we didn't care. Our first night alone, and we had cuddled and kissed all night. Carol was menstruating and it seemed to be a big thing to her, not just because she had no napkins and had had to wrap a white cotton petticoat between her legs. That was bad enough, but the red stain looked shocking and I wondered if it was normal to lose so much blood—did she need a doctor, what should I do? Carol didn't want me to see her stained underwear— she was almost pretending it wasn't happening, that the blood would somehow disappear, but now in the sunlight she crumpled her petticoat up and dumped it in a bin. Before I could offer she just took some money and went off to a chemist.

Sitting alone in the stable I looked around and reality closed in on me like a fist. Inside its palm the darkness chilled my bones, and through the clenched fingers and broken palings of the stable the sun poured in. The morning sunlight turned our first hideout into a backyard slum. Okay I'd have to get her things, but did she have any, and were they back in her mother's deserted flat?

It was warm in the stable now. Old planks had been thrown over bales, others up against the walls, to hold the roof up. I couldn't see any nails; it seemed as if the planks were just held by gravity.

Carol came back and it all changed. She found a little

brass stove over in a pile of junk; it was only a metho burner the size of a can of beans. She found a billy and boiled up some tea using an empty can of baby powder as a cup. It was the best cup of tea in the world, I told her. She said: 'What's the matter with you? I know it's as rough as guts, but it's better than a cup of warm piss. Look, I'm not stupid, just stop treating me like a kid.'

I realised that she was a stranger, that she was this strange and unusually beautiful girl and that I was with her somehow, it was another life. I had stumbled into reality but I didn't know how to talk. I couldn't possibly have told her that I thought she looked beautiful there that morning—most of her make-up had smeared away, and her hair was black, mucked up and wild-looking. She had tied a ribbon around her head to cover her hair but it was falling out, overflowing. I thought of the song my father sang every time he got drunk: 'The Girl with the Black Velvet Band'. All I could say to her were practical things like where should we go, would her things still be in the flat, would it be dangerous to go there? We had to find out; Carol needed a change of clothes, and we would have to get her stuff out of there somehow.

The morning sky had clouded over and a light rain was slanting down across the lane. We went out to the Ford, but it wouldn't start, so we pushed it down the slope until the motor turned over and it started. The rumbling purr of its V8—a burble, like a metal heart kicked back into life with a flutter—was music to our ears. We jumped in and I drove down to the stormwater tunnels at Tunks Park. We had to plan our next move.

I parked the car and sat back, looking out over the little bay. I looked at Carol; she looked out at the water. I looked out into the grey morning and thought, this is all a mistake, a foolish mistake. I should have taken some things from home before we left, before I charged out—food, something to cook with, a frying pan, camping stuff. We decided to go back to my place first, raid the kitchen and pick up my clothes, get whatever I could—my fishing knife, some tools—then we'd go back to Carol's flat and see if her things were still there.

By 3 p.m. we were at my place, picking up some crazy things from the kitchen on our way through the house: a packet of flour, cans of creamed corn, beetroot. Carol juggled them in her arms. I went into my room, opened my clothes draw where my mother had put a couple of packs of Peter Stuyvesants (she even knew my brand). The cigarettes were neatly folded between one of my white work shirts; that wrecked me—what a touch. She knew I was broke and I'd be wanting a smoke, and I felt terrible. I thought that she must really like me to do something like that, it was so considerate. I thought, oh, I just can't do this to my mother, it's all a mess. Then I saw Carol's face in the half-light reflected from the street, and she was unearthly and so lovely. I thought, oh well, it's either my mother or Carol, so I kept going, putting my stuff together, a thief in my own house.

We drove under the Harbour Bridge down to Blue's Point Road. We parked across the street from the building Carol's flat was in and walked over. It was a dump; an old red-brick block, there was garbage in the hallway and empty beer bottles on the steps; it was a dark warren. We thought they might have changed the lock, but when we got to the door it was open because the lock had been smashed. Inside there was a thick, dreadful smell; the electricity had been cut off and there was no furniture, just tea chests. Carol gathered up bundles of her clothes in an old suitcase. We backed out, left, then got into the Ford, which we had to push-start. I'd run out of time to pay the woman I'd bought it from so her bikie friends would be on to me. There was nothing left to do but to head north on the Pacific Highway.

The Koori Pit-stop Interlude

WE had to leave Sydney; they were after us, the child welfare people. Carol's mother had dumped her, my parents wouldn't let us live at home, it was all hopeless. We were in love, we couldn't live without each other now, we were all each other had, it was just me and Carol.

We drove straight up the Pacific Highway in search of peace, heading for Queensland; we were going to set up a flat. I'd get a job as a pastry cook, and we'd live right up there on the Cape. We were serious, not just another couple of kids pissing off; we were going to get married when we were old enough to do it without consent, we were going to show them.

We left Sydney and made it to Woy Woy, Budgewoi, somewhere like that, and we ran out of petrol. We knew we'd have to resort to milking. We'd drive by night and sleep in the day. We were in one of those towns—Wyong— with all those weird hedges and lawns, hedges shaped like animals, wallabies and things. They were big round hedges like huge green balls, and the lawns were all so neat, so clean, like they'd been vacuumed. I picked the neatest one, jumped over a hedge shaped like a castle wall, walked across the lawn and found a hose. I cut off a length, five yards or so, with my fishing knife, then off we went, me and Carol, down the street dragging this hose like a tail. We filled the tank of our Mercury at a garage, then we wanted to get another four gallon drum extra. I was syphoning away when the hose slipped out, then Carol just grabbed it up and started sucking. She'd never done it before, and she nearly coughed her heart up. She swallowed a mouthful of petrol and there she was right outside this garage spluttering away as if she was having some terrible kind of fit.

We had to scarper, we had to get out of there quick. I shoved her into the Merc and drove off like a maniac to find a tap or something. Petrol burns your lips and mouth and gets in your throat and chokes you up. The fumes make you high and you lose your timing. We found a tap after a few miles, at a beach-side shower in a park. Carol jumped straight under, clothes and all. The sun was coming up out of the sea; everything seemed brighter, the colours looked brighter; we were near one of those concrete buildings with signs saying MEN at one end and WOMEN at the other. By the time it was light Carol was showering naked under this stalk of pipe with the shower head bent down at an angle, her clothes scattered around the iron grate drain. I wasn't too worried; it was Toukley, or Tootley—one of those beach towns with a funny-sounding name. It was like a ghost town at that time of the day. Carol changed—by now she had taken to dressing in my clothes, mainly jeans and loose shirts and an old army coat when it was cold. I washed and showered as well; the petrol was through everything, our lips were cracked, our mouths were burning and Carol said her throat felt as if it was on fire. She was making jokes about being a dragon, but I knew she was really suffering. We weren't too good at milking petrol; we were failures as Bonnie and Clyde. We drove to a beach with sand dunes and found some cover, then we ate some butter, cried together and fell asleep in each other's arms on the big back seat of the Ford Mercury.

It took us about two days just to get to Newcastle. We didn't drive in, but went right around, through Swansea and out around a lot of big lakes. By this time the money was gone, the car was starting to play up and we were feeling pretty sick and sorry. The generator had burnt out—it wasn't recharging the battery, and we had to steal a battery from a car wrecking place. I got in over the back fence, found a battery, picked it up and then dropped it and spilt acid all down my legs. Then some kind of dog started up barking, so I grabbed another one and took off, jumping over through the hulks of dead cars with this demented hound from hell howling after me from behind his wire. I threw the battery into its mounting, kicked the Merc over and off we went.

The car was stuffed; it was blowing smoke now like a smoke machine, leaving great billowing clouds of black smoke in our wake as we rolled on out of that terrible disaster. We'd been going to service stations along the highway asking for old sump oil; now and then some grease monkey kid would say sure, help yourselves, so we'd pour it into the big old side-basher motor and big black globules of it would slurp out from the oil jugs. The old Merc used as much oil as it did petrol I think, and we were getting pretty frayed at the edges. I thought that any minute Wanda's bikies would come swooping down on us for the money I still owed on the car. Something had to give soon—either the bikies or the cops would swoop. The police would surely be on to us by now, following our zigzagging trail of milk money robberies and petrol milking raids.

I was starting to crack up and Carol just wasn't talking anymore. She just sat there in the front seat staring into the future of no flat, no escape across the border, no Queensland. Then we saw this place outside of Taree: Purfleet—an Aboriginal reserve or settlement. I didn't know what it was at the time but it looked okay, something more like Mooney on the Hawkesbury only less threatening.

I swung the car over into a dirt road; the old Merc was hissing and percolating away and making terrible clunking sounds deep in its block. We drove down the road and three young Koori boys came out, saying: 'Gooday. 'ow yas goin, what's the score?' These boys obviously loved cars, especially a car like the Merc. They liked Carol, too. She hit it off with them straight away. They helped push the car in and asked if we were shootin' through. 'Have ya left 'ome—you fellahs, are ya 'ungry?' I told them we were on the run, told them the car needed fixing and asked for their help.

They liked the whole situation and one of them said: 'Yous are safe as long as ya stay 'ere'. They said we'd have to park the car out of sight and then took us back to their place. We went in and their mum cooked up some mullet and gave us some bread and a cup of tea. Carol struck up a conversation with a girl called Shirl—they were about the same age and just went straight into a big talk. I was introduced to Billy and his brother Brian Jackson. They were friendly once I mentioned Gosford Boys' Home; Billy had been in himself. Before long we were pissing ourselves remembering Cheezy Borgese and Chookie Fowler—I had once been Fowler's houseboy, but I didn't mention that. Billy had been one of the verandah boys in One Company. We'd been there just two years apart— Billy had gone in just as I was going out. It was our version of the 'old school' sort of thing.

'So 'ow long's ya been on the outer now, straight?' Billy asked. 'Hey, you want some fun, like a real deadly muck-up? We'll fix yer car later. Come on, we'll go jaggin' mullet, get some more fish. We'll 'ave a big cook-up. Sounds great. What's the hitch? 'aye, you city fellah too long now, common—ya gotta git some tucker for ya girlfriend? Whadya feed 'er—aye nuthin'—bullshit aye!'

'Yeah, sure, but me car's fucked.'

'No worries, whatcha reckon we fix him later? We've got a ute, so's let's go git some mullet.'

I checked with Carol, and she was going great; she was in with Shirl fixing some clothes and stuff to wear.

'Well, leave 'er. Wimin's business,' yelled Billy from the ute, an old Chev. He was outside already, revving shit out of the motor; it was blowing smoke and sounded like a machine gun because they'd taken the muffler off. 'Come on, jist git in.' We were off, down the road over to the Manning River.

It was the time of year when the big bullies came travelling upstream, so they would be so thick. Billy reckoned you could almost walk over the top of them there were so many. What they'd do was to jag them out with a twenty-pound line with a treble hook and a big bean sinker on the end of the line. Their lines were wound around big old Alvey side-cast reels; they bound the reels to a long length of rangoon cane. They hurled the hooks out fifty yards, then started retrieving the line, and every two yards or so they'd throw their shoulder behind the rod and jag as hard as possible. Twuuunnngg, hissssss, the line would tear out and then they'd scull-drag them in.

This was called a Ned Kelly rig, and with it you could jag a box of bullies in half an hour, beautiful, big, bull-nose mullet. The trouble was that it was illegal. The local fishing inspector had been waiting for the run; he'd been after the boys for weeks, and unbeknown to us he was parked on the other bank of the river, waiting.

We got stuck into the fish straight away. We hooked and jagged and pulled, filling a fish box every fifteen minutes or so. They were beautiful-looking fish, bullies in top condition like little silver torpedoes. We would fill one box and then take it over and dump the fish into the back of the ute. It was about a quarter full when Billy noticed a light. It just flashed for a second, he said, and he knew it was the inspector and that we'd have to piss off, because it wasn't worth the risk.

The fishing inspector had tried all his tricks to catch poachers, but so far he hadn't got Billy and he needed to catch him red-handed, with the fish as evidence. He was close, only two hundred yards behind us as we grabbed our rods and the fish box and ran to the ute. He flashed his big torch right on to us, and we all jumped in and Bill drove off. The ground was slippery with mud and the wheels of the ute spun, slowing us down, but we were just a bit faster than the inspector could run. He was coming after us, flashing and shouting, stop, stop, you little buggers, but he just couldn't catch up. I looked back through the window and noticed we hadn't locked the tailgate properly; it had swung open and fish were spilling out behind us. We were burning across the park, the fishing inspector just yards behind shouting, flashing and dodging the slippery trail of silver pouring out from the back of our ute.

We hit the road and the tyres bit into the tar, the wheels screamed and we were away. We got back to Purfleet and we all piled out; we discovered that we still had some mullet left in the fish box—just enough for a good feed. We sat around an open fire for the rest of the night, eating fish and damper, singing, drinking and talking. The story of the fishing inspector was told, over and over, and each time it was better.

Two weeks later we were sitting around and somebody asked 'Tell th' one, yu know, fishing' 'spector one, the mullet story, good one again.' In those two weeks Billy and Brian had helped me to fix up the Mercury, cadging parts from one end of Taree to the other. I think some might have fallen off old trucks in the backs of wrecking yards, but it was fixed and the old motor was purring like a beauty. We had to keep inside Purfleet most of the time. Billy's mum was starting to worry about all the parts that had just kept turning up out of the blue, and she also noticed the cops were patrolling around the place more often. Carol was getting restless and I think she thought we might end up living there forever. I was getting on fine with Billy, but he was starting to flirt with Carol and she was playing up to him; it was time to move on.

A Sugar Bag of Trout

WE woke at dawn and found we were parked up some old winding track in mountain bush, some logging trail; we'd slept well in the car all night. I got out and looked around, and saw that the ground was covered with a lace of frost, the bush ghost-like: white, and drained of colour. I walked through the frosty grass and onto a trail in the scrub, an animal path, some kind of wallaby probably. I edged around a big yellow boulder of sandstone and found a clearing. In it was a beautiful creek with a pool like a little jagged mirror; it was bordered with frosted paperbarks. It was all silent and so still, then I caught a glimpse of some small black thing which floated over towards me and then started swimming. I looked into the clear pool and realised it was a platypus, which was feeding, floating up and ducking under—it was incredible.

I ran back to the car, scraping my arms on bushes, grabbed Carol and started dragging her back to the pool saying: 'You've got to see this, you've just got to see it once.' I knew Carol wouldn't have seen anything like it, coming from Ireland, and I knew she'd never even been to a zoo. We got there and I stopped and made her creep up to the pool. 'Go on, carefully, do you see? Look, it's a platypus.' She looked at me like I'd flipped. 'What are ya talkin about? What platypus, I don't see no platypus.'

It had gone. The little pool was still, empty, like a mirror with no reflection. 'Okay,' I said, 'let's wait. It might come back, it'll be worth it.' After half an hour I realised the platypus wouldn't come back, but the place was beautiful like an enchanted scrub. 'Let's just sit awhile. The sun's coming up now, so let's just enjoy it,' I said. I knew Carol almost believed in the platypus; she wanted to, I could tell—it was the first time on the journey that she had wanted to think something positive. She was disappointed, though. I tried to describe the platypus: I told her about its duck bill, its tail like a little shuttlecock bat, its spurs, its fur, webbed feet, but the better my description became the more unbelievable it seemed. They are the strangest animals in the world, I tried to explain.

By this time the sun was warm and it was wonderful just sitting there; the birds were singing. I told Carol about lyrebirds, whipbirds, birds of paradise and then my favourite, the Australian bustard, the bush turkey. I told her how they scratch furiously wherever they go, how they build huge mounds of dirt for their eggs, all by digging and scratching with their powerful legs and claws. I liked the way one would turn up every now and again and find someone had built a house on an old mating ground, then how the bustard would set about digging up the lawn, destroying the garden, making these great mounds everywhere.

Carol didn't like the sound of them. She said: 'What if one comes when we have our place in Queensland, what if I make a beautiful garden and one comes and rips it to bits? They sound like horrible things,' she said. 'I don't want one, they're awful.'

I teased her about them more, then she grabbed me and started wrestling. We rolled around in the damp grass. The frost had melted, the sun was quite hot and we got covered in dirt. We went to the pool and washed, then sat dangling our feet in the water. We tasted it; it was sweet, sweet mineral water, so we drank and filled up a bottle. Carol came back from the car with a heap of receptacles, pots and billy cans she'd taken from doorways, things for the milkman to fill with fresh country milk. She was saving them all, she said, for our 'flat'. It sounded wrong, well, a bit sad like a dream that mightn't come true. I think Carol still believed that we would do it, that we would make it happen. She was so determined, so fierce with hope. I didn't say anything; I used her dream to keep my spirits up. This had happened often as things got more difficult, and it was the only thing that had kept me going at times. We filled up everything, anything, that could hold water: billy cans, and bottles with wooden corks I made from bits of branches whittled down with my fishing knife.

The next night we were back on the road, cruising up the New England Highway. We drove and came into what seemed like fields of water. These great fields, which were paddocks of wheat or maybe lucerne, looked like lakes. It felt like we were driving through a divided sea. On each side of the road these huge lakes of moonlight waved slightly in the night breeze. It was so beautiful, so lulling and seductive that I just wanted to keep driving; that night I could have driven on into infinity. It was a wonderful landscape—it seemed to wander, to move with us, and the moon was on it all.

We came eventually across some strange white buildings, long things that looked like bunkers, and we couldn't work them out. They were surrounded by cyclone fencing, and they had outside lights although they were dark inside. We thought maybe we could find some food in there. We stopped the car and walked over. Carol climbed the fence and I followed. We looked around inside, and saw a big series of ponds, ten ponds like big swimming pools except shallower. I noticed something flick, then on the surface of one a fish ring. I looked in and saw trout, big fat trout— I couldn't believe it. It was a trout farm, one of those places where they breed them and then release the fingerlings back into the streams. That's what the white buildings were, State Fisheries, and the ponds were the hatcheries.

There was no night watchman. This was fantastic, we would eat again, we would catch our dinner. Carol jumped in and tried to grab one, but it wasn't an easy task; although there were hundreds of trout, they were slippery, and impossible to grab with your hand. I got in and we tried to round some up in a corner, but they just slid through our hands as we jumped around after them. The night air was freezing and we were wet, and after another ten minutes of jumping, lunging and grabbing handfuls of water we stopped. We stood there in the moonlight like drowned rats. I said: 'Wait, I'll go and get something from the car to catch them with.'

I opened the car boot and I spotted some old sugar bags, I thought that maybe by punching holes in one it might work as a net scoop thing. It was worth a try. We tried again, but it was still hopeless. I got out of the pond and walked around looking for a smaller pond or something, then I saw a sluice-gate handle, a little brass wheel that you wound to let some water out. I thought that if we let some water out the trout would be easier to grab, so I turned the handle but nothing happened. I turned it again, not realising that it was some kind of hydraulic mechanism. With one more turn the whole sluice opened, and although there was a grill to keep the fish in all the water went gushing out. It rushed at a tremendous rate, a powerful force, a wave surging out and rushing into the next pond. It drained our pond, leaving all the trout flagging about in the slime on the bottom. It was a fearful sight.

I couldn't think straight and Carol was yelling now: 'Get 'em, get the little fuckers.' There were hundreds of them, big fat rainbow trout all flapping and flopping and leaping up into the moonlight. Carol was grabbing them and throwing them up onto the concrete walkway. I picked up a couple and broke their necks in despair. Carol shoved them into the sugar bags.

I said: 'Carol, it's no use, we've got plenty, they'll only go off.'

She was excited, and said: 'No, no, we'll keep 'em, take 'em to the next town, sell 'em, sell the lot've them.'

'Who's going to buy them?' I asked.

'The milkbars, the fish shops, anywhere.'

We would get sprung, we would immediately be caught, I tried to explain. As soon as we tried, as if they wouldn't know. This little episode would be an outrage. 'We have to get out of here, Carol, fast. We'll have to go at least fifty miles or more, we'll have to hide up for a week or so, wait until it all blows over. They'll be after us, everywhere around here for miles.'

She said: 'Okay, then we'll just keep 'em for us, we'll eat them ourselves, make another camp back in the mountains. I'll cook 'em.'

I explained how they would rot. 'They'll all go off in a day or so, we'll have stinking trout everywhere, in the car, stinking trout, all through everything, and we'll have not only the burning, lip-cracking, foul-smelling petrol through it all but now this as well, this new smell, this terrible stench, the foul odour of putrid trout. Dead fish.' It turned into our first big fight. We drove off screaming at each other. Carol had a sugar bag full of them; they were on the back seat, some of them still wriggling.

CAROL/ROBERT

Correspondences

◆

Carol Luck's Interrogation

SHE sat on the mudguard and let her head roll forward; black hair fell down her face, but she didn't care about the screaming going on all around her. She just wanted to keep moving, to get back into the car and go. Anywhere, what did it matter, as long as the road hissed behind her. She'd be leaving, leaving things, leaving her life without having to die. Her greatest pleasure was just to sit in the front seat of the Ford Mercury, the street lights flicking by, a blurred fiery fence. The V8 thrumming—yes, they thrummed in a real particular way, a sound, a feeling and sensation no other donk could deliver. She knew Fords, V8s, models from 1939, 1940, 1945 and then in the 1950s the Customlines. They had a '45 Mercury; Ford stopped making them in 1949. The first '50s model was the Single Spinner, from the bullet-like shape in the grill; after that there was the Anniversary Model, the Twin Spinner.

Carol was quick picking up on things, things that mattered, stuff she was interested in. She was thinking, if only she was moving now, in the front seat, the valve radio crackling static in the dashboard, static from out there, the night. Yes, just to go, to move without thinking about having to stay right in the head, to leave the ordinary day, the land of the living dead without the pain of entering through into the unknowable world, or zone, or the whatever of death.

Carol knew that she thought too much, well, thought about things no one could ever know about, like death. *That's the trouble with you, you think too much*; she remembered her friend Jessy would tell her that. The trouble with me, she thought—yes, thinking those black thoughts, thinking—yeah, my trouble. She smiled a dark smile under the street light.

The police were bouncing their flashlights off the face of Robert; he was trying to confuse them, trying to act confused—well, he's good at that, acting innocent, confused she thought. Then one of the cops kicked the front wheel of the Merc. Something about the tyres, it was always the car. Always something to do with the car bringing them undone, some detail, something they made sure they found, they noticed—a defective blinker. It was their way of destroying her fantasy, a defect, a 'defect notice'. She picked up on the meaning of the word; it flashed with the trappings of authority, something to remind her of her place. Knowing her place and knowing she knew it—she fed on the irony.

She knew it was a word from her way of living: defect. It didn't belong out there in the world of day-to-day-living, where nothing was a 'defect'; out in the rows of brick houses, where everything seemed to work, where the police came and corrected defects, came to take the defective away, the broken laws, broken people, kids going wrong. It was another intrusion, another way to keep her from her dark thoughts, her death dreaming, another method of forcing her into some activity. Their way of putting some blockage between her being and the abyss.

Then she was in the police car, a cop either side of her; she sat there and the smell of their beer-soaked breath enveloped her. Between them, squashed, and not just physically. One of them with the lecture, the other with the snide sex in his teeth, biting the end of every second word. She left her body and drifted above it all for a while, but there was nowhere to go, even in her head, and the day oozed in through her ears.

She wanted to be able to break down, sobbing and quivering, but nothing broke from the flood of her pride. She surprised herself as she became aware of such a quality. She spoke the word out loud: pride. Without tone, just flat as if she had no idea of its meaning. She decided she liked it and said it again, this time emphatically: *pride*.

'Whatdyer mean,' said the cop with the red face, 'pride? Pride—you wouldn't know what pride was if it grabbed ya by the tits. Pride! What a joke! We'll show ya what pride means when we get ya back to th' station.'

Carol closed her eyes, took herself back to the morning of the day before. At dawn she had washed herself with Robert in the Fyshe River. She remembered the sweet taste of the stream and made it cover the air around her in the police car. The pure Fyshe water bubbled in around the obnoxious cops, washing away their foul odours and invisibly bracing their complacent psyches.

'What da ya say, wacher say to that?' Red-face menaced. 'What are ya lookin' so smug about, yer little slut?'

Carol was beyond the touch of his voice; her mind backed off, jetting through inner space like a squid away from a predator. She looked down over the entire field of her life, seeing it all at once. There she saw that these two cops were terrible, yet not so terrible at all in the scale of things, in the incredible meanings her life consisted of, the whole picture. They were two specks in the rushing stream. What interested her was that there seemed no edges to it all, no mouth at the end of the surging tide, just the stream gushing on.

She was looking for an end; where did life finish? There seemed no stopping it, no end. There in the cop car she could see her life was beyond just being a person, even that she, as a living being, was alive, and that from this life death was impossible to picture, impossible to even imagine. She understood then that this ride with the cops was nothing but a small illumination, although she was pleased she understood it as such; she had never previously taken in a vision of her life in this way. She knew she would be able to continue night rides, she could move on after this intrusion and maybe death would be less inviting. She'd continue on with her dark thoughts, she'd think them and maybe at times let some headlight cut through, some spark from the engine illuminate a phrase or two.

Carol knew that she'd survive the night and that there'd be plenty more for her to drive through.

My Dearest Carol

I have written endless letters to you. I've lost count of how many, most of them in my head and others written on pages like this 'letter-form' I am writing on now. They leave one every Tuesday but I have crushed many of them up and thrown them into the can. Others I have just left and not handed them in for posting. We are allowed to write one letter a week, every Tuesday when I come in from the exercise yard I find one left on the shelf in my cell. I pick it up and put it on the Bible, sit on the bed and stare into the blank form and think of you. I think of you every day of course, I'm sure no day has passed without you entering my mind at least once. I try to summon up the courage to write and send one of these letters to you but I end up writing to my mother instead. This one will make it, I'll send it but I wonder if you will ever see it anyway. Maybe the Vicar will not pass it on. He will probably burn it or just throw it into the rubbish— are Vicars honest about these things? Do you think he might decide he is protecting you by not letting you become exposed to the moral danger I am supposed to be to you? Who knows, maybe you wouldn't want to read it even if he does pass it on. You might just read it and not want to answer. I don't know what you feel about these things anymore. It has been a year. I've been here in Maitland Prison for six months and before that they kept me in Long Bay for what is called Classification, trying to find out if I am crazy or likely to be violent—I'm not allowed to go into any detail about it here because of security—you wouldn't want to know anyway. They have an Officer who reads and censors all correspondence. They censor newspapers as well. Sometimes it's so bad it's funny, you get a page and there are great big holes in it where they have cut out some news item—it makes the paper seem much more fascinating than it would be uncensored. Why am I telling you all these ridiculous details?—probably because it's all very bleak if you let it get to you. The other prisoners are horrible, mean and ignorant except for a few rare ones, usually homosexuals, who have been outcasts and don't want to inflict suffering on others. They are also more sensitive. The days flow into days and time stretches on before me like an endless highway except there is no scenery along the way—no trout farms, no rivers, nothing but wall. Carol I love you more than ever and it is a deeper love—the only way I can get through the day is by trying to imagine your face, I picture you in my mind's eye, your black hair, your eyes—I wonder if you ever think of me? What is your life like now, how are you living, what have they been doing to you? Have they brainwashed you into being a nice Christian country girl? I can't imagine it. There are so many things I want to know and it's all impossible—I'm only making a guess at your address but surely there is only one Church of England Vicarage in Tenterfield? I can't tell what is real anymore, I try to sort out the story from my memory.

I have told some of the other crims the story of our 'escape' to Queensland, how we ended up in that little border place called Texas. I change the details each time, it depends on who I am talking to—each time it is different, now it has become so confused I can't remember what really happened. It's terrible when I am alone in my cell, not knowing the difference between the reality and the story. It's even more disturbing because when I go to sleep I dream about us. You are different in every dream— sometimes you speak in a language I can't understand, some kind of wild Irish. It sounds like a talking-song, not only because of the way you are pronouncing the words, the words are not English—it's Gaelic probably—though I've never heard Gaelic spoken. You are always leaving me in one way or another, at times you float off into the distance, other times you just turn your angry back and walk off—I keep watching for ages but you don't even turn around to see if I'm still there. Sometimes you speak without sound, your lips move and yet there is no sound in your voice—I try to answer and the same thing happens to me—I try so hard to speak, nothing comes out—then I wake up covered in sweat and shivering. I try to remember the times we made love and then think maybe we didn't even do it—except for the one time, the time of the platypus, the platypus you missed seeing—I know we must have made love at least once—after all that's the reason I'm in here— for making love to you—for carnally knowing you—it's strange language they use isn't it—from the Bible. O Carol

I miss you so terribly and I'm not very strong in being able to handle it.

P.S. This is the end of the form, it's all the space they give me, this double page—please answer. Even if it's a Dear John, anything, just to know, that's all I need—one way or the other.

Yours Forever,

My Dearest Carol,

I'm convinced now you haven't received my other letters. I've been reading and also completing my education by doing a Leaving Certificate by correspondence. I am permitted to send long letters now because I am doing the course. This letter will still be read by one of the Officers for security reasons. I can say anything really as long as I don't describe what goes on in here other than my personal thoughts. I thought I'd make this a letter called All-The-Letters-At-Once, to make up for all the letters I wrote to you but didn't send. I call them Ghost Letters. I write you a long letter and it turns into a confession or a statement, into something strange. The next morning I read it and wonder who I wrote it to. I am no longer writing to my mother, in fact I am no longer writing to anyone except for a visiting Jesuit Priest who came here a few months ago. His name is Father Hopkins. He is a wonderful man and we discuss music and poetry. I gave him some songs I had written and he said they were more like poems. So now I am reading poetry and I have decided to become a poet. It will take years of study, first I have to pass my Leaving Certificate and then I will go on to do an Arts Degree—but it will take ages. I am reading a lot, any poetry I can get my hands on. Also books about great artists like Vincent Van Gogh—I have read a book about him called *Lust for Life* and it has changed my life. I am reading poetry by Shelley now and a book about him called *Ariel*. Carol I feel closer to you now than ever. I have a feeling we are somehow a part of each other. We have existed before in another life as one person. Maybe a woman. Maybe a man. It doesn't matter, when we were separated our soul was torn in two and you went into a woman and I went into a man. Inside we are still the one, though each is a separate half, we will never be whole until we are together again. Two souls in one body. Does this sound too strange to you? Don't worry I'm not going crazy, this idea has been known to people for ages, yet only poets and mystics seem to talk about it as far I can tell. Shelley talks about it. I think that's where I first discovered the idea, then in another book called *No Man Sings*. It is the story of a Greek poet, Sappho, who lived on an island called Lesbos. It's all about the feminine side of things, the side where poetry comes from I think. I will tell you more when I study further. I find it easy to understand, it all seems natural to me and explains a lot about things I like and how I live—well how I would live if I was not in a prison—although being in a prison is like being trapped inside a body—except the terrible thing is—it's not your own body—it's the body of some terrible black beast. You have no control over anything except your soul, even keeping your soul intact is difficult. If I can manage that I will survive this place. It's impossible to believe though that I will ever be let out—although it's only two months now before I am going to be released it may as well be two hundred months. Every day is an eternity and each night is a season in hell. Anyway—that's not what I want to tell you, this letter is a freedom, in fact it is the only time I feel free—while I am inhabiting this page, this world of my letter to you. I feel I can be anyone I want to be here, except I don't want you to misunderstand—I'm still the same person yet I'm able to change as I go in this writing. It is a wonderful feeling as long as I don't look out from the white page-world— and see where I am, even the window in the top of this cell with its bar across the night. I want to be a part of you again, and in being a part of you become whole again. I don't mean like together as we were on the road on the run, or even together making love—together as I said before—two souls in the one body—though we can't actually be one body—we can be two souls that mingle, two souls together in each separate body.

All these thoughts about souls and love seem wonderful as long as they are contained in this Ghost Letter of mine, this is not real this page-world, though maybe it is the only place now where you exist. I mean have I made you up? I don't know. Do you exist as a real person out there in some strange farm in New England? Do you go to Church on Sunday? Have you become somebody other than the girl I knew on the road, in the car? Does that wild girl running between ponds in a trout farm spilling a trail of iridescent scales behind her on the grass exist only in my memory? Are you really the girl in the story I re-tell every Saturday to the other prisoners? I describe you as they play poker in the exercise yards, or the cages, the details mingling with the fact—what a word—the fact of this love? I remember my arm around you as we looked up into that sky on the mountain range, where the Fysh River rushed and its gushing power sprayed us with a mist of fine sweet water. We looked into the Milky Way and the turbulent night sky with its comets and shooting stars— and then the moon came up like a great orange circle through the dark fingers of the gum trees, the branches had skeleton hands and their fingers moved; 'Do trees have bones?' you said, and I called for the Tasmanian Tiger and for the Snowy Owl. We were free for a night. Now if I look away from this page, I see a grim cell and think how I'm having myself on. I think I'm making our love into a myth because I can't believe in God—it's because I'm probably going crazy with prison looniness—and yet the dreadful thing is that I feel clear, sane and somehow cold. Bemused. I reach out and trace your face with my finger in the black cell air.

I have a new friend, and would you believe it, his name is The Finger. He says we are all alone each one of us and gods and muses are like having a bet two bob each way. The Finger is a card player, he has never lost a game of poker in his life. He is in here for cheating, for fraud or something, but he wasn't cheating, he just kept winning so they framed him. The Finger says he was born with luck but it is his curse. He says I should send you one of these letters I have written. I've told him all about you and my Ghost Letters. The Finger said if I post one and you answer it he'll put a bet on it. He says he can't lose but he won't tell me which way he is going to bet—*one*: that you answer and say you still love me; *two*: you either don't answer or you write me a Dear John. With his luck he can't lose. They bet on everything in here. I feel a strange sort of comfort because I don't really have to make decisions anymore, it's all like clockwork, endless, terrible, circular—yet there's no centre to anything, you don't have to believe anything, you just let the days revolve and take your life forward, a day at a time, chipping away. Time is a great block and you just chip away at it.

It is the next morning and the light coming through the cell window bar is just bright enough for me to read what I wrote last night. Carol, I really can't remember what you look like anymore. Maybe I have made the whole thing up. Maybe I have made you up, maybe you really are just a muse. Poets write for their muses but do the muses ever write back?

Police Confession: Tenterfield
2/12/1958

I, Robert Adamson, born 17/5/1943, of no fixed abode, pastry cook, on or about the 20th May 1958 did meet up with Carol Luck who was hitching a ride on Willoughby Road Crows Nest. I drove her in my vehicle, a Ford Mercury Sedan, to my parents' home in Neutral Bay. After talking to my mother it was clear she would not agree to Carol moving into our house. I discussed this with Carol and suggested that we both leave and go to Queensland together. I would find work there as a pastry cook and we would get a flat. We left Sydney and drove up the Pacific Highway, along the way we stole petrol by milking it from other cars, we also stole pots and other receptacles for holding milk along with the milk money. We broke into premises with the intent to steal and in fact did steal some things and food. After many days on the road travelling by night and sleeping in the car on the side of the road or in the bush by day, we got to know each other very well and became lovers. I asked Carol to marry me one day when she was old enough to do so, until then we would live under false names. I did not know her age, Carol was confused and frightened by her terrible life with her parents, who finally abandoned her and her sister. Carol lost count of the years and in fact she lost count of time altogether because of the conditions and situations of her life moving from country to country, from place to place. I thought she seemed older than myself in some ways and she did know more about life than I did at the time. She looked much older than she was also because she had developed earlier than most other girls. Along the way we made love in the car and if you want to call it Carnal Knowledge I suppose that is what it was but it didn't feel like knowledge to me it felt like love.

Signed & Witnessed: Robert Adamson & Senior Detective Wallace Fowlie, Vice Squad.

CORRESPONDENCES

We are your circumstantial evidence.

BARBARA KRUGER

◆

PHOTOGRAPHS BY

JUNO GEMES

Robert Adamson and his father Harry in 1946.

Betty and Harry Adamson go to town.

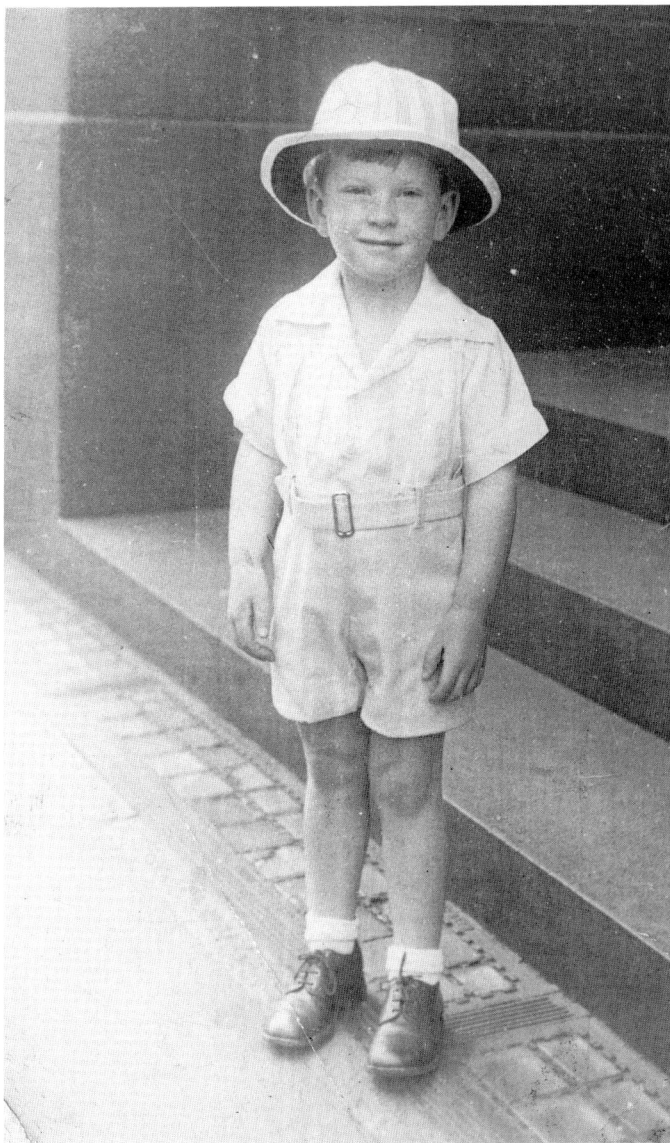

Robert Adamson aged four.

Henry Thomas Adamson (1887 – 1986)

Family fishing trip, 1953: Robert Adamson (second left),
his father Harry (centre) and grandfather Henry (right).

The family in 1955, with Robert Adamson holding
a cat in the front row.

Robert Adamson aged eleven (right) with brothers
Richard (left) and John.

Family picnic at Balmoral Beach.

Robert's racing pigeons.

Rick the Trick stands with Robert beside bird cages and
the chook-house containing the Paradise Rifle Bird.

Rowing in to Mooney.

Roadstory, Hell End

Boat With An Empty Mind

Boat With An Empty Mind

WARDS
OF THE
STATE

◆

PART TWO

LOOSE TALK

It is life that we are trying to get in poetry.

WALLACE STEVENS

◆

LOOSE TALK

The Tightly Written Life

ALONG the curb, 3 a.m. so cold, so warm, the seasons
ball into one if you think, look back
the night's where you find your drug
the only food that counts is in somebody's eyes—
the rare ones, unclouded, focused
touch without burning, that deep steady pause
recognition. Though usually it's
self-delusion, or some spark of a dream cut loose
from the nightmare.

Street Kids

THEY speak for themselves in a code
of unmaking, slurred vowels
and a burst of laconic gutturals
to fend off action—what's
uttered between them could pass
for warning or affection.
They rehearse for nothing;
these are the Serapaxed mornings
of sun burning the blue
calligraphy of skin tattoos.
The desolate laminex corner nook
in the *Alnite Angel Bar*
is their beauty parlour—though
don't drop your guard
and exploit their habitat with pity
or condescending, there's no
language here for conscience
or visual concept for 'lifestyle'.
This vernacular putters between
voice box and burnt lung.
Their poetry, drawn with a spray pack,
describes a stark economy of luck
and mocks the slick jargon of cash;
this anti-commerce has made
its way from dank boardrooms

in stormwater drains, bypassed the grim
service of dole queues, has sidled out
into the light without style, with nothing to say.

State Ward Sonnet

THE mess hall by shimmering glass reflected
on porridge bowls brown sugar flavoured

Winter gets under the nails of a boy
who'll darn his socks on his hand machine

His behaviour's a new art to annoy
and he'll pat dry yellow blisters between

his fingers with a cloth tucked in a sleeve
day dreams get suppressed weeding beans

So bring back those cruel marching songs
Company One is better than a hole in solitude

He rocks back on raw haunches for long
enough to weave more letters in his head

mother comes out spelling 'other' tattoos
five separate letters on each finger in red.

Albion Street Children's Court

THEN you're up before The Beak
he frowns under his dumb wig
but waits without a word
through the social worker's rave
I eye the bothered police
the Court's as dark as Noah's Ark
your head spins out of sync
and your eyes are like shovels
your brain's a dump
but you cop it sweet because
there's nothing as bleak as a red Beak
You hear as your life
gets carried off in years
on the words they slot into
a machine moving jaws of the law
so's to shut you up so you can't squeak
and to lock you away so's to clean their streets.

Hot Dogs and Alchemy

SHADOW walks the wharf on a line of sun
through the silver air of Woolloomooloo

by the calm harbour, she holds a rose
in a bunch of crushed cellophane

Along by the drunks lined up like stumps
brown paper wrapped around their plonk

Shadow sits in a corner to cut and cook
a spoon of speed with a flame

from her flickering plastic Bic.
Don't picture this image of Christ's fish

spiked in ink on the back of her hand:
take this as a scene within a scene

Shadow's just turned seventeen today—
she tries to dress like death

and succeeds, a black leather belt's slung
across her chest studded with skulls

the size of sparrow eggs; she has a way
with style now every day's her carnival

Seagulls squabble between the marker buoys
and the hot dog stand, a pack of mongrels bark

in the lane. O meaning, sweet Meaning
sings Shadow, will I still find you when I look?

Petrol Sniffing

A red shell on a yellow can: a joke
before experience—and all the money boxes

left in a corner, jagged, open.
The children bumping soft foreheads

in morning steam; a prickly scent trickles
from a cap, hands too young to shake

tremble; the heavy metal fumes sink home.
We have tomorrows to eliminate,

though who knows how long the brain
can take the fingers of vapour

that soothe the pain—Any bad dream
dissolves to the touch of a rubber snake

that dribbles its menthol from cracked lips.
Give it names and call us sick

but your real drugs cost a sister's lunch,
and the whisky's in your sin-bin;

Southern Comfort's for that lucky bunch
who can afford their own extinction

in style; oh, sure, it's a luxurious joke—
though you can't joke when you're flat broke

It's a plastic bag when you're on the nod—
don't think we can't see you getting off on misery.

Expedition to Reality

A crimson neon scrawl; the biggest word in town
hovers on steel scaffolds—the ad-man's
manifesto, illuminating our way through
   the blinking city.

We travel under glass, along tunnels with air
cleaned by machines, then pumped back
with a cold bite; our breath contaminates
   sterility with life;

Us? A tight pack of sleek children, in your
language, who fight your cool prose
by clicking a finger, to indicate some
   meaningless symbol:

well, less meaning we intended. We make
images to bounce off your glazed eyeballs;
as we are thinking this, you may be
   speaking of plague—

it has been said, that too is meta-speak:
images of words, your broken language
with shards of our meaning chipped from
   our father's block,

with images of mothers transferred from cave
to factory wall. Each jinx we manufacture
is scooped up and transported back to
   your spiritual life,

or what's left of it. We have taken 'family'
to re-invent ourselves as your real
children, we have even learnt to escape
   your sad affections.

We trail behind you in supermarkets and snigger
as you fumble money at the checkout, though
take stock: don't take us as threats who flow
   like an invisible boa

underground, through the clouds of sodium fog,
   deep in city gizzards.

Social Realist

THERE'S no one in charge but I do
the talking, there are some
things you could put into words
just in case, not that you'd
ever use them. This is no flash
racecourse where the punks
have resumés—sure, there are
times I might get out of it—
but just give me the nod
and I'll speak with a shocking
accuracy just to pester
your cynical awareness with raw
fact. These impossible words exist
in a desert called lifestyle;
it's difficult for me
not to resort to mockery, waste
more paper: write and they
call you Headspace. Up the road
there's a movie on, directed
by some fashionable bent German—
it shows how gullible
imaginations fall to a designer's
'look', this destructive
nymph splashes black right across
the screen, yet somehow she's been

pasteurised to get them in.
She's what passes for a muse
and is loved for her
elegant implausibility. Though today
she is head down in astro-turf, blown out
posing for B-grade pornography
and who knows what city
she is in, head shaved, beyond time
squinting through the new conjunctivitis.

Another Graveyard Shift

A zone you say is not a place for work,
no corners, tables, yet cups of everything
even tea; like this zone's a blade
    blackened by heat,

to chip at your feet, putting colourful sparks
on your heels if you try to make
a step to break away; it's a zone to say
    leave brains at home.

No decisions-allowed-here-zone, so shuffle
up Pitt Street in the heavy-going dark
it's harder going backwards when you look
    light in its face.

Though you notice the crack of pinkish glow
is dawn coming straight through a block
made of slabs of glass and steel, just then
    you get a whiff:

it's last night's sweat curdled with scent
from your ex-lover's clothes, so for now
it's a mate from the lost boy's patrol to show
    the quick way back:

straight into the gates of the flat factory
out here suburban dockyards aren't fake—
they tick you off as you clock yourself on
    a two-shift bake;

and the kiln's fired up by a mum whose son's
more terrible than his father's last thought
though the shift goes on and you leave
    smelling of work;

as you walk down the road to a shopping mall
where your head drums up new kinds of pain
stretching your temper till it gets to feel
    like a rubber glove

with its fingers gone; you've got some
kindness left but it's home with Mum
under the sink near Ajax that washes the walls
    like any other day.

Empty Days, Empty Nights

A loose shoe drops onto the pavement
Jim's down with a ripped shin
from kicking in windows,
half-baked attempt at a grab—
A double reflection of two men
runs over the sheet glass,
the trouble's Jim's little brother's
too young to get cut up—
though he's the one with a blade.
That's how, then one night
Rat flips and the idiot drips
blood down warm on Jim's new strides.

A can of rum & cola on the table
Jim sees nothing—he's in heaven
under neon, drifts through a memory—
melancholy in his bubble
of remorse and alcohol. She looks
at his bruise, Pam slings a slug of whisky.
Then tells me I'm old fashioned
because I've got a Dad who never used.

Sign This

I will sign anything in case someone
notices, my name means nothing
in reality, no bank takes it seriously
and shops call for the police
at the sound of it, the police see it
written on reports and throw
them into the shredders; my son rubs
it from the envelope he uses
to carry his father's photograph in;
my name is shit so I won't plague
you with the details, I can't give it away
and it follows me through hell,
and when I was talking to my mother about
funerals and stuff I started to think
well what are they going to put on my grave.

Loose Talk

A can of Victorian Bitter beside a thick
tumbler. She flicked a black look
straight through the rag of her fringe,
one eye blue from being punched.

She rocked back, muttered from a chair:
'We're all creeps when the chips are cashed,
sick to get rich, even grabbing
with our mouths. Oh, sure, talk can be

a kind of money. Floating in the air.
Hey mate, you're looking real crook,
no wonder, drinkin' that shit.' A bubble
breaks and pocks the creamy froth, a spark

of light flecks the red line of her lip.
On the fake wood wall, the *scene of Italy*—
and by its torn paper lake, a detail—
Alpha's emblem in the alpine atmosphere.

A page ripped from the menu, a lipstick
script, it's her best classified.
Who's game to say what they imagine
she might dare? It can only get worse

the waiter thinks. Tell her something now
she doesn't know. O, shit, yes—a word
that's umbecoming to us feminists—
muses of paper, words and printer's ink.

She takes a knife out from her purse;
the handle's pearl, see if it twists.
All this rhetoric's fit for Rimbaud's hands.
Give back his beer, rancid old misogynist.

BOATMAN OF THE GLOW

Like the sea fishing/Constantly fishing/Its own waters.

L OUIS Z UKOFSKY

◆

Rabbiting—Hill End

A feather circled down into the misted scrub,
my father's shadow waltzed over
river craters. In the back of our 'rabbit truck',
his old red Bedford, smothered in furs,
I looked out as he walked those riddled slopes.
Long pocket nets dangled from his shoulders
he rubbed blood from the ferret's pelt.
Out the back of Driscoll's paddock
our camp fire was a triangle of luminous red air
in the thick of the night's black felt.
We watched a pair of fox eyes stare
then turn red streaks in the moon's cream.
Every light had a life behind it,
or was fire making life for my frostbitten
dreams? Now looking back through the same fence wire
forty years and I still care
for all those paddock spirits imagined here;
as ice-blue stars sink into the eroded earth
the river hisses its feathered serpent's breath.

Boatman of the Glow

My grandfather walked through twilight
down Blue's Point Road, lighting lights.
I only know there were poles
and a long thin stick was involved.

He is the reassuring figure who comes
up from the wharf's glow. His oilskin
would catch your eye, reflecting sparks
from raindrops in his collar's gutter.

He talked so easily, though he'd mutter
about the one thing he had it in for,
The Gale, that's any wind at all.
A breeze shaking out the garden wattle,

a wind from bushfire thick with ash,
a simple draught, he'd call 'a gale'—
Some of the last words he spoke
concerned the blast: 'No fish, no fish

at all, it's been blowing a week—
even in the kitchen, full of goats
against the blow.' He'd have his horse
out in the shed, feeding on the oats.

'The wheat pollen and bran, we'll lose
the lot, just think of the cost.'
While outside the long black turds
his peacocks dropped, steamed in the frost.

Underneath the house in a cave of time
he'd hoard the hours the clocks had lost,
in tins and boxes, charms, a talisman
made from the knuckle bone of a fox

that fed on his best Rhode Island Red.
He kept jewels from jewfish in a box
of dovetailed cedar with joints so fine
he used a glass to admire the craft.

He'd rattle a red tobacco tin
of oyster shells, to call his tumblers in;
his racing pigeons once carried notes
to Mrs Barry when he had his 'fling'—

Then, as the old gentleman, he'd walk
my wife out on his arm, politely saying:
'If he does you wrong, then bugger him—
darlin', you'll do me, I'll be your bloke.'

The sun catches a shard of broken glass,
dissolving time in a prism's spark:
today he shines an old buckle. 'Those cows,
we'll muster them, and they'll be lard

for the soap factory.' He loved a lark
with words that nudged at darker rhymes—
and played with time for almost all
his century; I see goats still in a dark

kitchen with a fuel stove, the horse
he rode across the Harbour Bridge
was named in some old country song;
while outside the gale blows on forever.

It picks up those old peacock feathers
and fires them, ceremonial arrows
killing mocking voices in that tide
some think is time, my grandfather's hour

has come, tunnelling from Blue's Point
to Mooney Mooney, in a great blaze
of gas light illuminating his backyard
with its sink of lime dissolving

myxoed rabbits and dead water rats—
while around the fence mad peacocks
bail up chooks. The old man chats
to a grandson; a makeshift incinerator

burns fiercely, he stokes the grate
with fishing licences that have expired,
old examination papers nobody could pass—
they laugh now as it all incinerates.

My Father's Boots

ALL here, a brain gone soft with fear;
memory? Now don't aggravate the rot.
Look, a kingfisher's blue flame in mist.
The sun stirs mud's bacteria to stench.

Swamp, the wives, kids, unkind relatives,
under my skull there's landscape not
so pretty. Though in this weather I twist
in away from lighting: being burnt

alive aside, it's the illuminated beach.
A lucid vision of those journeys to reach
a lover at the end when surf was right.
That's where I'd find my father—

he'd chip clay from his hobnailed boots;
I'd lie in the room and hear that sound
each night. Words would fight
to escape my head but my lips were tight.

A child turns to rocks, and then turns
them over: underneath the worms and crabs
all try to scuttle back. I found
dark solace as they writhed like silent words.

La Mancha Sunsets

THROUGH the clear day a hot wind of dust
cuts into eyes and lips as it gusts
through azalea pots and snapdragons
along the path to Dolly's caravan.
Behind *La Mancha* is a lake locked off
from the sea by a spit of scrub;
it's shallow water where nobody goes by day.
At night Dolly looks out
as holiday prawners with tilley lamps move about.
She gazes into the black pit
where her husband took his drunk rage
three summers ago and didn't come back.
Every dark of the moon she looks,
remembering council workers
dragging Joe's stiff up into the blue day.
Dolly sucks at a bottle of her cooking sherry
and looks into the black lake,
where tiny lights the shape of tadpoles move about.

Night Lesson

I watched right through dark,
stooping over the night
until a school of gar
shot through the mesh wire
silver liquid arrows flying
through wheels of white
phosphorus lights,
and in a circle of cold fire
they churned the dark glass
of the surface into sparks
of crinkling cellophane scales,
falling through mesh
and flaking underwater snow.
My corks were lumps
that bobbed about slowly
as the next shoal hit
oblongs of the bull-nosed mullet
crashing into my wall net
a strange drifting fort
above them in three dimensions
bombing these silver roses.
My boat had now become
an old gumboot stuck in mud.

I uncurled my stooped body,
stretching out into this world
bleak with death and cold
except for those great bull-noses.

Before the Hook

'GITCH yer friggin hands offa me glass;
you should be shot yer mongrel, spilling
a man's breakfast, flippin' idiot.'

Coon Dog grizzled out from his face,
quick cracked lips in line with a left ear
without a lobe. His rum slapping about

in one hand and a beer into the other.
'I been 'ere forever now and th' only nit
with gut t'say so—stayed through the wars,

two of 'em, an' drank me way through
every fear that lobbed, an' they threw
everything, cause I didn't give a brass razoo.'

Coon Dog grabbed my arm, whispered low:
'An' what'da want from life old mate?'
I said to make a go of fishing—he took

another shot of rum then cackled: 'Arr,
ya drippin' mad. Ya wouldn' know a pike
from a pelican, shockin' way to make a quid.'

His face was black with sun and tar
and he clicked words from brown peg teeth,
then waved about a webbed and speckled hand.

'I was created on the river, did yer know?
One morning, k'pow, I just appeared.
Me father took me in cause no one else would,

and then I grew up overnight they reckon.
I fished with me hands before I wove a net,
then when I wove I stitched it with twine

tanned with the bark from seven trees,
then finished off with woolly-butt.
Me nets are invisible to fish *and* Fisheries.

'You weave on the moon's first quarter—
they all reckon it's bullshit, but let 'em
weave by day then watch and the fish flow out

straight through free. You get th' nights
when there's breezes, well, just forgit 'em.
Glass, that's what ya shoot, black crystal.

'The mist'll roll down from upstream, it looks
like fur the colour of bushfire smoke:
don't make a sound, then shoot, you'll tell.

'See if it's bullshit then. Dawn an' silk
ripplin' with a thousand translucent fins
bucklin a bay. But, mate, you stick ta books.'

Blood Sport in the Half Light

As they left safe moorings
oyster poles were white
exclamation marks
on a slack tide. Language
was my conscious way

of paying some kind of human toll,
though the act dances
now forever into the sun.
Words that passed
between these crazy men

were not music to squawking gulls,
salt air got polished
by wings and floating hair.
Take this for granted
then, words are just one way in.

Here we enter by the side
of a fish, great golden slabs
of meat with scales
and dorsal spikes
shooting up through a tailgate.

The bait fish was rolled on
the skipper's palm
with a rainbow trail
like a snail's. A warm fillet flutters

down through ocean's
liquid crystal, an underarm cast
sends the hook sailing out
from its carbon fibre longbow;
others follow

from rosewood centre-pins,
plastic casters, old burnt cork.
A rod tip twitches
with a shuddering yakka,
then doubles over;

the sound of some great hand grabbing
up yards of the tide
and ripping. At the stern
the skipper leans back
and stacks on the pressure.

A line of foam breaks
on the wake as black fins
cut through a surface bulge—
his line's now stitched
to a sea alive

with the scattering whitebait;
he is playing God
in his head, yet with his left hand
swings a stainless flying
gaff.

The Tomb of Language

La negation est liée au langage—Maurice Blanchot

LIVES and words; what's between ourselves
and language, words, those husks
empty of meaning though somehow signs—
   let me point to

the bitterness of a man, who in the face
of extinction, living on a peninsula
in a toxic harbour, stares at the moon
   carefully awhile

has it drift arteries of his existence.
So for the tomb I offer my dead grandfather,
feeding poacher's nets onto Dee Why's
   unpolluted sands—

while in Homebush, my father drags his lungs
through the brickyard kilns to pay
the endless rent. Let him offer you some
   distilled bitterness,

drunk by the blind hoons pissing
after the six o'clock swill, my brothers
mumbling their lives away in the scores
   of weekend football.

My mother as she turns her head away
from the magistrate at Children's Court,
while I watch my memories as they dance on
   a chook house roof:

the kind of narrow patterned truth
you get from a man who's never told it.
So I offer this half-learned magic,
   some call it proof

against the fool's gold in a trance
induced by the morning glories
smothering the primrose—transformed
   as The Great Work?

Well, something in language then; for you,
whoever you are: mulberries, the luxury
of a fuel stove and your grandmother
   mottled in flour.

THE BIRD-CATCHER'S SONG

Y-a-a-ss, Y-a-a-ss, Y-a-a-ss, Y-a-a-ss.
PTILORIS PARADISEUS

◆

Over Our Roof Winds

CRISS-CROSS and bring metaphoric
odours of war hung with black hawks
of metal. Our hearts are sick
though by tender acts of kindness
each day we love each other more
as we move in a space beyond talk
where fools think they can express
some meaning from Official Death.
Generals flicker in the small screen
as we watch a burning child crawl
toward the hole its mother has become.
Outside our window, in the green
sub-tropic zone, birds and insects hum:
making it all the more obscene.

The Bird-Catcher's Song

BECAUSE it is my work, to catch bee-eaters,
and you love watching the bee-eater's flight,
I will catch one, feed her for you; so many
    bees she will die.

Because it is my work, strange work I know,
I will catch you the delicate firetail finch,
and for you feed her flames so you can see
    fireworks of love.

Because it is my work, against life I know,
I will catch a brolga and let her dance
the dance of death, so we can live and dance
    in the flames forever.

Because it is my work, it buys food and clothes
for our son, I will catch an eagle hawk,
let him swoop to the lamb in a dance of claws—
    a kill to feed love.

Because it is my work, terrible work with guilt,
I will catch you a lyrebird to mimic this song,
then my patrons will never know who is singing
    these songs that kill.

The Boat with an Empty Mind

1.

NINE cats float their eyes above the shore;
each pair globes, lit from within,
scatter as I suddenly move and kick over
    an outboard motor.

Magenta's feathery clouds uncurl the sky.
This is no boat, a roaring head of metal
growls and spits as I toil with a rope
    coiled in slimy loops.

I slip it into the belly and stand back—
call you high in the light, beckoning
with hands, darling I say, quick look
    it's all gone black.

The surface mirror dark as a cat takes
a flying leap to the white pylon,
misses and smacks into the river's flow
    it flies up the totem,

exploding with salt. We end up alone
again; a crew of two we rumble over
the low lying mud flats, gaze into our
    prehistoric mountain,

with windows there ablaze with light
you paint 'strange figures' with your eye.
We splash through a jet black tide
    watch freeways climb

in concrete scrolls up into mountains.
The outboard motor coughs, we slough in mud.
Out from Coleridge darkness a lifeboat
    empty by our side.

2.

We kissed and it turned winter. Our kiss
will be a site for others, collecting stars
that shoot by, lovers will gather, some
    beckoning to promise.

You follow through trailing trinkets, lures
artifacts to sculpt and charm my soul,
back from this vast black mirror speckled
    stars in parchment

and rock face: remember the steady elders
making this crossing, in dugouts sewn
with wattle bark, they notice kissing lovers,
    chuckling, they know.

A Morning's Kill

Down old sandstone steps in dawn dark
I cut through silence, rods become
antennae to guide me through a park.

Beyond hedges, a black mirror of bay
circles the shore; no ferry's arrived
although I hear the coughing spray

and dribble of the wharf's plumbing.
A yellow light swings over the pontoon.
Cold air cuts to the bone and numbs

my fingers as I tie the tackle knots.
I bait a hook, cast out, the prawn plops
onto the ginger surface, fine nylon

monofilament arches over with the bait
then begins to sink. I feed a yard out,
pull back; a bream glides in, takes

its prey and disappears. I jag on line
now kicking with fish. A cut hand
stings and yet I smile at the shine

down there where the silver shape turns.
The fish flapping, gasps on the sand.
Thoughts flicker and, half-forming, burn.

Prayer

MEMORY has my life in its silent flickerings;
what words can remain offerings after
they have been spoken to more than one lover?
 Take these phrases,

in this winding line here with the sorrow
I can never bring alive; these hours arrived
and although I have struggled for them they are
 spread before me.

Tonight they are somehow thanks, from where
I cannot imagine, although there is no place
that I cannot imagine, thrumming here now
 under phrase making.

A rhythm for the child I did not give life to,
music's life, little enough I find in ways evoked
with the words that I place here precisely,
 a craft of meanings.

Mary Durnello's Song

MARY Durnello wanted to write poems
she had composed with graceful ease
in the shape of cylinders of glass
that spoke with a tone growing out
from hours spent alone with thought.
She told me of her forthcoming book,
no title page, no index or epigram,
just cylinders of shapely thoughts.
She preferred her thoughts to ideas,
as she spoke explaining song's flow
unfolding a glowing thoughtful tune.
How melancholy it becomes to invoke
such promise in Mary's sad absence;
how she'd scorn this masculine myth
woven from such bright intelligence
without her body's savage presence—
and its concern for darker matters.
Wallace Stevens said this was proof
of the spirit's mannerism—utter
sense, though with his lighter touch
as if it didn't hurt quite so much—
but at the end I hear a curt rebuff.

Kenneth Slessor Dancing

WHENEVER he looked through windows, in life
or poetry, he'd wake that other self
inside ourselves, then send it dancing out,
  the man who isn't me—

he'd say, there's the true dancing dandy,
sliding those Italian two-tones lightly
over any evening's whistling floor, no doubt,
  just twirling elegance.

He'd go dropping the pretensions even more
into light of those imagined nights,
a devil laid bare, who might be there . . .
  Old ghost, the cock,

who cares? The words fell from his dance:
the toes would never be hurting, he'd toss
off the form or shoes, and shed his skin
  like a garter snake;

then skinless, over the periwinkles, rocks,
dancing in lapping tides, no shoes or socks—
he laughed at the Grey Nurse in the surf
  doing a jig or two.

Then back in his flat on Billyard Avenue
he'd watch the harbour and along the shores
his invisible improbabilities would renew
   his wobbling libido.

Gazing through his window one morning saw
the milkman, Ken listened to him chink
chinking bottlers, put his fingers to the glass
   tried to rethink

his choreography, he jerked back with a pang,
in pain his hand crabbed open, to pass
through glass a dancer's circle back to dance:
   ends song as it began.

Looking Out Sideways
for Barrett Reid

THROUGH haze waves figures wobble about
on a sand-tattered shore; I talk
as we look out, saying there's
one freedom more inviolate than any other,
it comes to us when we trust what we
truly know. Now what we know
is poetry, a power as difficult as a bow
with the arrow going off to kill,
even though we don't want blood on our hands.
All those wars and arguments rock
in our skulls, making a tight
but silted kind of harmony. A flock
of gentlemen move into our view;
they are wearing shirts with lines
from poems emblazoned on to their backs,
their flight is a wonderful clumsy sort of foxtrot.
Now children come running out from fishing shacks
along the beach as if they knew these fellows
were escaped black and white butterflies out of lost poems
from *The Movement*, like Philip Larkin with
a long line of false epiphanies strung together and thrown
    onto the page.

Outside of Delacroix
for Barret Reid

OCEAN cupped between sky and earth, the sea rolling
out through the Heads, two people stand and gaze;
it's in the mind again as usual
though here from my window
I look up through actual hills and see water
or water's shape on the sky
and want to say to you
yes although we have made it up it's real
let detail convince careful readers
we want to get beyond the speck of blood
on the collar, the ash smudged on the sleeve
where someone's butt has rubbed
this chip of fingernail the stumps of white hair
growing in clumps on the edge of the chin
Ah *The Pacific*, how you know now what old poets mean
when they say let's watch the rim awhile
and rustle up a phrase or two
Two cane chairs standing empty by the side of the sea
their checked shadows embossing the dirty sand
invisible hands gesture in the dusk
We are happy and lost in the meaningless sound of verbs
and toss them off like stones
let them skip out in a sentimental wash of ink
abstract and obscure

the way we like it, yet vague
reverberating with little edges of meaning
just enough to keep a child from wandering off
and yet, who knows what death means, what matters is
    pain
as you cross over the water.

What Love Takes

THEY are being killed as we speak love
on the Alps or red flecks in a shallow valley

In towers the fire watchers gaze obliquely
inwards and dream death far from them

always happening as we become lovers
as we feel our privilege and speak softer

it happens as we smooth the crumpled sheets
in polished air of our gathered walls

Though don't look up there is no skylight
no window open to the dying out there tonight

More Grief
for Martin Johnston

HAVING survived the days turning weeks
into a flat beach of years, unable
to write poetry I wrote designer verses,
though stuffed them in behind the books

on my desk shelf; at the dinner table
my mind bled its invisible ink
onto imaginary sheets of thick *Fabriano*—
I called my cups of tea my 'drink'.

With tight lips I rhyme all this out
away from the poetry confessional, to show
it is too late to make guilt or doubt
a worthwhile subject; and even though

I could make the pain feel tangible,
pain too can be self-indulgence to the hilt
when it's not specific, and plain talk
more bullshit when suffering's not particular.

I cursed Mallarmé as the keys spat
words *and* spaces; incomprehensible phrases
seemed sweet music as the tv news
turned even Eliot's verse libre into backchat.

Then Martin died, on the table *The Rock*
by Stevens sat unopened; a kind of sense
four poems in, said: Lebensweisheitspielerei.
The stale grandeur of annihilation answered back.

The Kite

GREAT mud flats surrounded Lion Island
tides had ebbed away etching lines

in a spit of white sand that stretched
from Juno Point to the Lion's bushy head

the sky's horizon illuminated by rescue flares
on the sandy bar a boy flew a kite

in the steady westerly it dived and wove
its tail in air, its paper bows fluttering

like translucent butterflies on the Matterhorn
in Switzerland sailing through Vladimir Nabokov's last
   dream.

The Symbolist's Daughter

A stroke of oil paint ripples out the bay
there is no one for miles in sight
A memory swims, flitting about
then enters the picture
stinging a patient reader on the cheek
reading her book on a butter box
in a trailer park in Woy Woy
Back here in a village near The Entrance
there is a dark pool where we stoop to drink
our memories drip down our shirts
and tongues remember the taste of Swan Ink
Grief is the tall figure out there
walking the sand dunes heading for the water
he sings a thin song its lyrics
barely audible—it is a mournful tune
drastic with salt his head is under the beak
of his cape, his shadow is thrown
by the moon's first quarter
So take up the memory of a dead daughter
enfold it in a handkerchief with embroidery of names
then crumple it and throw it out to sea
Dark clouds obscure the sickle of pink moon
I push forward to you, through this, my hand a flesh
  flower

Sonnet for Christopher Brennan

HERE'S poor Chris playing the drunken mage,
a crumpled uncle who's hunched on the bar
across from his staff club table;
(he drinks himself an invisible cage)
Later in the afternoon he visits his room
and sits singing a delicate German tune
each word of it pockmarks the rancid air.
One foot taps at a letter on the floor
but he struggles to untangle his coat
now turned straitjacket by his chair.
Mary, his cleaner, late at night is gentle
as she sweeps around his sleeping bulk.
On the floor a black calligraphy fans out
pages of Mallarme's letter, his fallen mantle.

Violet Singer Takes a Ferry

AGAIN caught ideas of Brennan grow
in a flat moment on the tram
at memory's edge, one image flows
over the harbour in sonnet form.
A foot comes down on a twig
that snaps on the steps leading down
to the wharf at Mosman's Bay—
I float in rich fog on a pontoon
and a little wind my arm makes
travels down the cotton sleeve of my
shirt, chilling a sticky rivulet
of sour sweat; morning crumbles like cake
and here's Vie, the ferry crew part—
she walks on saying the one word
over, a short rough syllable, her last
utterance, though not his name.

Montsalvat Burlesque

THE coast road passed through our heads
at 2 a.m. with Robert Harris navigating, using
Frost at Midnight as our street Directory
   Coleridge by dashlight—

Our first hop was a truck-stop cafe, tables
spun with our foul-paper book-launch talks,
in stainless-air we found the coast was clear
   when a waitress turned

to listen to those lines that whispered
of frost and its secret ministry, out there
with no need of wind or slipstream,
   weaving a sub-text

through Dylan's singing on the tapedeck—
How nobody mocked our canticle is wonder:
it was light that turned the tables. Robert
   measured every syllable

pinging on the window of the Big Sheep's eye
as his voice-print told the way. Then
sure as trouble, a bike roared around
   The Wall Of Death

ridden by a leather jacket dancing empty
of its hoodlum's body. The highway
kept thrumming white elegies while the V8
    hummed its tight tune

balanced by modern instruments, no slapstick
gear-shift. It proved the Redex worked
a placebo's magic compared to new synthetic
    lead-free petroleum—

the memories full of laminex knocked over
and tangled up in limbs. Now there's no
fist fights, it's first night nerves—
    a glowing tachometer

with its eyelash needle flicking into red.
In this town poetry's a bedroom occupation:
Hart Crane's bitter irony, his hash of noise?
    Slung up from the street

and called 'performance'! The truck's thunder
coughs up the new morning's dead: make
poetry of that, bottle it, package a product—
    target the Grief market.

Political Alchemy

THE Great Work is neither false or true
though survives time; it becomes a means
to understand the stone and live it too.

Religions stir with fundamentals, no new
vision appears to inspire our dreams.
The Great Work is neither false or true

yet constantly reveals us as we continue
to consume ourselves; we are not keen
to understand the stone and live it too.

Here science finds in rock the residue
of industry, this atomic ore can mean
the Great Work is neither false or true

when it burns the land it passes through;
yet there is something that may redeem:
understand the stone and live it too,
the Great Work is neither false or true.

Ode to Beckett's Death

TAKE back the day though there's no
one to say that to

for I would give the day away I am
so bad at words
& let somebody new spell out

words for the deal
(and who is making it
nobody can have gall enough to say)

Cleave these syllables
through the knot my tongue is

torn against the devil
who does not have to make them spell

words bunged into words
Grief yes give us grief for god's sake

Epistle from Stingray Bay

I put these words down, smudges on thick
oatmeal-coloured sheets, not the ship's
journal; for you and the children,
to look at, to wonder at language's wiles
and a game to sort out differences—
What I see and what I think I see: no trick
but this place stammers and beguiles
as flowers bloom our food begins to rot.
It's all savage to the eye, the slash and flick
of pinions governing the dense atmosphere
little ghostly doves fly up then spin
down into the bay like stiff handkerchiefs—
I play out my role, botanising on the deck
while the others, oblivious with rum,
chuckle and curse, invent new forms of sin.
My passion for weirdness must be insatiable,
my mother's words come back as I become
her description of me—a wasted freak
black in moods, a never-happy thief
desperate for anything she didn't know—
And here it is, a day where there's nothing
to go on but my feelings, the blue sun
of the day flowering with difficult vegetables;
a week-long southerly spikes the air
with diamond sharp sand—my skin's tight

around my skull, my head's filling
with images of you, beloved Shara, there
in our park with sandalwood and China tea—
your dark freckled eyes float in a stain
of lemon oil on the milky shoal of memories.
This is my reality, and Cook, raving, Stingrays! Ah,
stingrays, and the shimmering sheets of rain
falling on shallows, curtains carved from sandstone
Shara, my arch lover, who remains?

In our Time
after Miklos Radnoti

I live in the world at a time
when men have sunk to a level where they kill
for fun, then write books
boasting of their gross rape

I live in the world at a time
when the informers and corrupt officials win
Medals go to the athletes on steroids
while our modest philosphers are ridiculed

I live in the world at a time
where if visionaries become eloquent
they are forced out of work
then driven mad can only smile at each other

I live in the world at a time
when mothers almost hope their babies die
as they curse the blood of the donor
though live on as they grow weaker on some new dope

I live in the world at a time
when in the blank face of all the burning
poetry seems ridiculous and poets dream
they might mouth the thin terrible words of Isaiah.

REAL DEADLY
RUBY LANGFORD GINIBI

I reside in an Aboriginal hostel called Allawah which means 'Stop! sit down and rest awhile' in Aboriginal lingo. It's very appropriate, cause boy! I sure need a place like that. I don't have a home of my own, I'm not whingeing, because there are thousands of my people like me, 'homeless' . . .

Real Deadly is a new collection of autobiographical stories and poems from the bestselling author of *Don't Take Your Love to Town*. Contemporary tales of urban Koori life are told with the humorous edge that has become the author's trade-mark. Memories of family life in country towns are wryly recalled, often in spite of the tragic circumstances that surround the Aboriginal experience. Real deadly stories of deadly times.

CRITICAL ACCLAIM FOR RUBY LANGFORD'S
DON'T TAKE YOUR LOVE TO TOWN

'The ultimate battler's tale . . . The life Langford has
lived in Australia is as close to the eyes and ears as print
on the page makes it.'
BILLY MARSHALL-STONEKING, THE *AUSTRALIAN*